THE LOST SERMONS OF YESHUA OF NAZARETH

SOME TREASURES WITHIN...

"As to the purpose of life: there are many. But the greatest is to reach a state of consciousness in which you have an inner peace which transcends mortality, making you one in spirit, thought and action with the boundless light of the Celestine realms." *Genesis 11:44*

"Never forget amidst the travails of mortality that you are sons and daughters of the divine Father and Mother and are connected in spirit to all living things both on Earth and beyond. You are radiant rays of light that can illuminate the deepest darkness." *Genesis 11:49*

"Seek to be one with the divine in your heart, soul, mind and spirit, and no challenge of the world will be able to overcome you." *Genesis 11: 71*

"You are in mortality to perfect yourselves; to overcome your weaknesses and make them your strengths; to increase the length and breadth and depth of your good character, even so much that your children honor you and hold you as their ideal, that many in need have been helped by your service, and that when you pass from mortality it will be remembered that to have been your child, or your friend was a blessing that lives on." *Genesis 11: 74*

"Therefore, ever seek to fulfill the divinity of your creation, ever doing good, ever welcoming the resonance of the spirit of Elohim into the bosom of your soul, ever seeking the perfection of your being in every way. This is your destiny." *Genesis 11: 125*

“Remember you are all sons and daughters of God and therefore are you all brothers and sisters in the spirit of God.” *Nexus 21:48*

“Recognize what is in your sight, and the feeling that is in your heart. Pray to your Father in Heaven for the light of understanding to expand into the testimony of truth, and then that which is hidden from you will become plain to you, and there is nothing hidden which will not become illuminated by the light.” *Nexus 24:42*

“The greatest treasure of all is to understand that there is an Almighty God in Heaven; and after all that man can do, there is still more that God will do for those who ask good things of them with a repentant heart and a humble spirit.” *Nexus 33:48*

“Elohim gave you the instrument of your body, but you are the musician that decides the music your life will play.” *Vivus 1:31*

“Seek to understand the heart and essence of Elohim and you will hold the foundation of good by which you may know the truth of all things of light.” *Vivus 4:115*

“Show by your example the higher path of life. You can fight against the darkness and thereby make enemies of the men of darkness, or you can bring the light and the darkness will depart. Darkness cannot bear light, and light can always overcome darkness if it stays connected to the source, which is Elohim.” *Vivus 23:42-43*

"Love is the greatest fountain of life you will ever know. Therefore let it flow from you in abundance by your thoughts and words and actions." *Vivus 26:52*

"Your eternity awaits you and whether you live in a world of light and joy and abundance, or a world of darkness and cold and hunger, depends entirely upon the choices you make every moment of every day; for you are the architect and builder of your eternity." *Vivus 48:57*

"Remember to be balanced in all things, and gracious, not judgmental in your toleration of the weaknesses of others. Seek first to perfect the temple of your own life before you judge others about theirs." *Vivus 52:82*

"And those that know and live my words shall be no more of this Earth, even though their feet may still tread upon it. For those who know and live my words shall be more than men and more than women. They shall be Celestines, who, staying steadfast in the light, shall someday become Adepts against whom the fiery darts of the adversary within have no persuasion, the forces of the world be they army or king, have no power, and to whom the body is the servant, not the master." *Vivus 99:113*

"And of all the words I have said to you, my brothers and sisters, these I say to you last: Love one another, even as I have loved you. In this is all the power of creation, all the power of the Elohim, and all the potential of the Celestine Light that is within you, waiting to shine unto the world." *Vivus 99:129*

Published by Kaleidoscope Productions
PO Box 3411; Ashland, OR 97520
www.kaleidoscope-publications.com
ISBN 978-0-938001-20-1

Layout and Design
www.3wizardz.com

THE LOST SERMONS OF YESHUA OF NAZARETH

Embrosewyn
Tazkuvel

SERMONS OF YESHUA OF NAZARETH

INTRODUCTION

These lost sermons of Yeshua of Nazareth were excerpted from the within the 800 pages and 459,000 words of the scriptural book the Oracles of Celestine Light. Most often these occurred as formal sermons where Yeshua spoke to large groups of people that had gathered specifically to hear him. Other times they were revealed just to his Apostles for them to understand and later teach others. In one instance, Yeshua's sermon was given to just one person, the Prophetess Yasvon, in Genesis chapter 11, for her to share with the people, both in her time and in ours.

Yeshua is most often known as Jesus in the modern world. But it is important to note that the Yeshua of Nazareth of the Oracles is not depicted in word or deed the same as the Jesus of the Christian Bible. Most of the sermons given by Yeshua that are included in this book are not part of accepted Christian teachings or canon of scripture, and are unknown to Christians.

Occasionally, there are some sermons such as the famous Sermon on the Mount that occur in both the Bible and the Oracles. But even in such instances the accounts in the Oracles are always more detailed and complete. For example, Matthew 5:6 of the New Testament reads, *"Blessed are they which do hunger and thirst after righteousness: for they shall be filled.*"

For anyone wondering what those mentioned in this verse would be filled with, the Oracles answers in Vivus 45:17, "*Blessed are they who hunger and thirst after righteousness. They hearken to the still, small voice within. With desire and action they seek to fulfill the will of God. They shall be filled overflowing with the Celestine Light that they seek.*"

Comparing the length, the Sermon on the Mount in the Bible is 107 verses composed of 2000 words. The Sermon on the Mount in the Oracles is 285 verses comprised of 11,146 words; over five times larger.

There are also occasional verses in the Oracles that at first glance are very similar to verses In the Christian New Testament, but closer inspection reveals a decidedly different meaning. A good example is a comparison of Matthew 5:17 with the Oracles of Celestine Light: Vivus 45:29-31.

Matthew 5:17, "*Think not that I am come to destroy the law, or the prophets: I am not come to destroy, but to fulfil.*"

Oracles 45: 29-31, "*Think not that I have come to uphold the law and the prophets, for I have not come to uphold any but those of truth, and to fulfill the promise of Elohim given to men to destroy those that are not. And there is far more to be trampled underfoot than to be upheld, for the teachings of God have been taken and the teachings of man have been given. I am he who is the builder, and I have come to tear down the feeble works of man and to restore the mighty temple of God.*"

THE DESTINY OF MAN

Excerpted from the Oracles of Celestine Light, Genesis: Chapter 11

Over a thousand years before Elohim the Son came to Earth, there lived in the city of Eridu, in the land of Kiengir of the two rivers, the descendants of one of the twelve groups of Savasi that had returned to Earth to bring back the light and lift the state of man spiritually and temporally.

2 This was the eleventh generation that had been born since the time the Savasi had first returned to Earth.

3 Quickly after their arrival, their ancestors had become one with the native people through marriage, and now they were indistinguishable from the Saggiga people who had come from the north generations before the Savasi had returned to inhabit and farm the rich land of the delta of two rivers.

4 Nevertheless, it was not forgotten among the descendants of the Savasi the stories of how their ancestors had returned to Earth to bring back the light, and though the Saggiga worshipped a wide variety of false gods, the descendants of the Savasi still remained faithful to the true light of Elohim.

5 Thus, it was that they still kept the ways of Elohim that had been taught to them by their parents and looked, with faith, to a prophet called of God to give

them the pure guidance, light, and truth of Elohim.

6 In her forty-fourth year, Yasvon the Wise was called by Elohim and confirmed by unanimous support of the Council of Twelve to be the new prophetess when Hasslamar the Astute died.

7 And it came to pass that the prophetess Yasvon fulfilled her calling, and through her came a wonderful book of scripture concerning the destiny of man.

8 These are the words she spoke to the Council of Twelve and the Children of Light on that day so long ago:

9 "Beloved friends, it is such a humbling honor to be numbered among you, and to speak to you this day of a great dream from Elohim that came upon me seven nights ago.

10 Many times in my dreams, I have spoken with the divine Mother and received her loving guidance that we might all become better than we are and continue to prosper in this land.

11 Occasionally, the divine Father has also come to me in my dreams, and his presence, though equal in love to the Mother, is so very different than hers.

12 It could be no other way, for we are male and female and have been created in their divine images. Male and female we marry and two become one; that in the two that are one there is a balance of love and light and strength and wisdom; that we and our children may always be blessed by the balance.

13 But seven nights ago, someone came to me in my dream who has never appeared before. Though the divine Mother and Father speak often of him, never had

I seen him or heard his voice. But on this holy night, Elohim the Son came unto me.

14 He told me that he had come to answer my question. In truth, I was surprised, though I should not have been, for I had been thinking much of late upon a most vexing question, but I had spoken of it to no one, save to Elohim in my prayers.

15 I had been pondering upon the history of man, from the times of Eden and Noah and our ancestors' travels to another Earth, up into this time in which we live.

16 It seemed to me as I reflected upon the history of man that time after time, there was a cycle of coming closer to Elohim and then falling away.

17 This could happen to one person in a lifetime or to a group of Children of Light over the span of many generations.

18 I contemplated how it could be possible for men and even Children of Light, in many times past, to witness marvelous wonders and miracles from Elohim and still walk away from the light and the joy that living in the light brings.

19 As I looked back upon the history of man from the time of Eden until the time we live, try as I might, I could not understand how it is that man never seems to learn from the follies of history and that the errors made by one generation, rather than being remembered as lessons of what not to do, are instead forever repeated by generations that follow, who become doomed by their foolish actions to suffer the same pains in mortality and immortality as their ancestors.

20 Why has this cycle never been broken? Is man so thick-skulled and dim-witted that no matter how many times he hits himself on the head with a mallet, he cannot comprehend what is causing the pain?

21 Why, throughout history, have men from Earth continued to war with one another and kill one another and do all manner of atrocities to one another, despite the evidence after every war that victory is hollow and that which is lost by both sides is far greater than anything won by the victor?

22 From our parents and grandparents, we know that in worlds beyond this Earth, this lesson has been learned, even by people more primitive than we of Earth are today. If it is so elsewhere, then why not here upon this Earth, with these men?

23 And how is it possible that Children of Light who have been blessed with knowledge and understanding and Celestine abilities above all others have ever been able to turn their backs upon the light and embrace the misery and loneliness of the darkness, even to participate in a level of war and destruction so great as to not be imagined by the men of Earth today, so great that those few Children of Light who survived were our ancestors who fled this planet.

24 But that which vexed me most was truly my incomprehension as to why after millennia of time, after repeated help and intervention from Elohim, after countless wars of pointless destruction, after countless lives of misery led by those walking in darkness, the state of man today upon the Earth is less than it was even at the time of our ancestors the Savasi, or of Noah,

or of the Edenites.

25 Upon the return of our people from the stars, we have given the people who were here on Earth new technologies that have propelled them to greater heights of civilization, but are there less wars? Is man kinder and more compassionate to his fellow man? Has loving service to one another replaced forced servitude and slavery? Beyond our small circle, do people have greater love for the temple of their bodies?

26 As was promised, our ancestors have been the seeds from which the new civilizations of man have sprouted, but that is simply a level of greater comfort for the shell of man. What seed of light has sprouted within the eternal spirit of man? Why after millennia upon millennia is man still in so great a darkness, still repeating the errors of every generation that has gone before, instead of learning the lessons and becoming greater in spirit and love than every generation that has gone before?

27 This was the question I have pondered and asked of Elohim. And in a dream, Elohim the Son came to me, and these are the words he spoke unto me:"

28 "Beloved sister of spirit, to understand the answer to your question, you must more fully comprehend where those who dwell upon the Earth have come from, why they are here in mortality upon this Earth and not another Earth, the fullness of the purpose of life, and the promise of life everlasting.

29 Mortality is not the first step nor the last, but a middle step in the eternal progression of man.

30 The Earth you live upon is only one of many Earths

that men live upon, so many in number that they are like the sands of the sea.

31 When children are taught in school, are the boys sent to learn beside the girls or the girls beside the boys? No, they are not, for the ways of the male are not the ways of the female; therefore, they are taught separately, in different manners, each for their greatest benefit.

32 Even within the schools of the boys and the schools of the girls, are there not still greater separations? Some learn quicker than others, and they are placed with their peers. Others need special attention to help them focus, and they are grouped with others like unto themselves.

33 By this, each has the greatest opportunity to learn to the fullest of their potential by being taught in a manner most in harmony with their spirit and studiousness, while the door still remains open to a greater harmony with another school if they desire something more in their life.

34 And so it is even in the hereafter, where each is drawn to that which is most in harmony with their spirit and their proclivities, be it light or darkness, but with the door always open to a greater light if they are willing to walk the path that leads to the door.

35 In mortality or immortality, it is upon this foundation of harmony that the eternal progression of man goes forward, that man may say, 'Here I am today, but with greater desire and efforts, there I will be tomorrow because that is the tomorrow that calls to me.'

36 Thus, man is rewarded in mortality and immortality with the harmony of his choice, be it light or darkness, and is always afforded the opportunity to seek a new

harmony and a greater light if he is willing to make the effort.

37 Therefore, think of each Earth as a school, and to each school of mortality upon each Earth are sent the students who are most in harmony with one another, be that harmony of light or harmony of darkness, that they will have the greatest opportunity to learn and grow and become more than they are.

38 Since the beginning of its creation, upon your Earth, some of the greatest lights of Heaven have been sent to be teachers, by precept and example, and you and the Children of Light are among them.

39 And they have been sorely needed, for your Earth has ever been filled with the malcontents of Heaven, those who, even in the life before life, were disruptors rather than peacemakers, doubters rather than believers.

40 Your Earth is their harmony. And their harmony is often war and destruction and abominations.

41 Unto these have you been sent and many other great lights of Heaven before you that you might teach by precept and example and raise their harmony to a greater height;

42 Not all the world at once, but line upon line, precept upon precept, example upon example, one person at a time.

43 Therefore, be not discouraged by the repetitions of the follies of man. Understand the harmony of the Earth upon which you live, even though to you it is disharmony. And know that despite the repetition of foolishness, you can change the world and bring it into greater light, one person at a time.

44 As to the purpose of life, there are many. But the greatest is to reach a state of consciousness in which you have an inner peace which transcends mortality, making you one in spirit, thought, and action, not only with your Earth and all life therein, but also with the boundless light of the Celestine Realms.

45 In this, you are in Heaven even amidst the trials and tribulations of life, and no challenge or vexation of mortal life that comes upon you can sway or topple you from your inner serenity.

46 Before mortality, you lived in greater freedom; no one sought your life, forced you to pay taxes, or compelled you to act against your beliefs. You did not have to squander the hours of your life laboring at that which you despise just to survive and provide food and shelter and clothing for your family.

47 In the life to come, this freedom will be even greater and your spirit will soar upon freedom's wings.

48 In mortality, you may not be confined in a prison of stone, but you are confined within the prison of your physical, mortal body and all of its weaknesses. You can fall sick or be injured physically, emotionally, mentally, or spiritually, and you can die. But so can you live.

49 Never forget amidst the travails of mortality that you are sons and daughters of the divine Father and Mother and are connected in spirit to all living things, both on Earth and beyond. You are radiant rays of light that can illuminate the deepest darkness.

50 In the life before life, you were as you are now: sons and daughters of God. But that knowledge was ever present, and because of that, many came to no longer

appreciate the great treasure that is their souls source, for the knowledge of it was always with them.

51 Now you are cast with the others into the darkness and forgetfulness of mortality for a lifetime. How can you best fulfill the purpose of this life? By reaching through the darkness and discovering yourself—the divinity from which you have come—and living the greater light which is revealed.

52 Love and nurture the temple of your body, for in that, you honor Elohim the creator. But do not forget it is but a temporary shell given to many imperfections, vagrancies, infirmities, disease, and death.

53 Nor forget that this very temporary shell is not you. It is only the physical covering of your soul for a breath of eternity.

54 Therefore, do not separate yourselves by the colors of your skins or hair or eyes or the beauty of your face or the youth or suppleness of your body, for these things are not you, merely an artist's covering to hold the brilliant sun of your soul.

55 The masterpiece is not outside of you. It is inside of you.

56 But for you to know and love your eternal soul and spirit, you must be one in spirit with the source of all creation, even our divine Father and Mother.

57 For by their command have all things come into existence, and there is not one thing that exists or has existed or will exist that is not from them.

58 You are a part of Elohim, and they are a part of you, even as you are a part of all that lives and all that lives is a part of you.

59 The cause for all of man's problems and sickness and sorrow is that the connection between man and God, and man and all life has been severed. Reconnect man to God and man to all life, in heart and spirit, and the man shall be transformed from darkness to light.

60 Return to eternal oneness and there is no place for strife, sickness, or sorrow, for man only wars with that which is not in harmony with his eternal soul.

61 Cease looking at the differences between men and women on the outside and instead remember and embrace the divine inner harmony that all people can have through the divinity by which they were created.

62 The resonance of this Earth has been dim and dark, separated from the harmony of Elohim that is bright and light.

63 Guide those in darkness to the light by precept and example, and many will resonate again with the light that is the source of their creation and eternity.

64 All the sorrow that comes upon the children of men, all the weeping, all the pain, all the sufferings, come only when man is separated in spirit from the healing love of the divine Mother and Father, which is an abiding peace and tranquility that overcomes all sorrow and pain and grief.

65 You were created before this world was as true sons and daughters of God to progress eternally that someday you might even become as our divine Mother and Father now are.

66 In the life before life, you were closer to understanding and being one and in harmony with that awareness.

67 Now in mortality, a veil of forgetfulness has come upon you that you may develop faith, that you might find your bosom welling up with feelings of overwhelming love as you connect again with your spirit to our divine Mother and Father, not from things that you see, which may be an illusion, but from that which you feel in your soul as it becomes one with all that is and rises to a new resonance as it recognizes the true harmony of its existence.

68 Remind yourself continually, until it is never forgotten, that your outer shell and the physical world are of little importance. Therefore, why should the challenges of the outer life cause you despair?

69 Be at peace and in harmony with your inner eternal soul and your eternal love and connection to Elohim and all that is, and nothing that assails you on the outside can affect your inner serenity.

70 It is your eternal soul and spirit that are of monumental importance, and all the mortal world has been created simply to help you more clearly find your eternal soul and, once found, to connect in a oneness of love to Elohim and all life; for the divine Mother and Father and all life are eternally a part of you, even as I am.

71 Seek to be one with the divine in your heart, soul, mind, and spirit, and no challenge of the world will be able to overcome you.

72 The men of the world seek to connect to the divine by making gods of kings and following elaborate ceremonies and rituals within a myriad of religions. In this, their spirit remains vacant, for you cannot find the

spiritual, which remains forever in time beyond this world, with things of the physical, which are here today and gone tomorrow.

73 Therefore, have no ritual or ceremony of religion save those of simplicity that move your heart and soul to connect in a oneness with all living things, a oneness with Elohim, and a oneness with the divine that is within you.

74 You are in mortality to perfect yourselves, to overcome your weaknesses and make them your strengths, to increase the length and breadth and depth of your good character even so much that your children honor you and hold you as their ideal, that many in need have been helped by your service, and that when you pass from mortality it will be remembered that to have been your child or your friend was a blessing that lives on.

75 As a Child of Light, your destiny in mortality is not to become a great leader or to be revered as a wise sage or a great healer, although you may become all of these things and more if it is your desire and focus.

76 But your destiny is far greater than any of these. It is a destiny given to all, but realized by few. Your destiny is simply to live up to the potential of your divine heritage and become as perfect in your life as is possible, given time and circumstances.

77 Begin with your attitude, for in this, you light the fires of your actions. Be sweet of disposition, praising of others, not critical. Be excited and curious, always looking to grow and expand your knowledge and good experiences.

78 Act with wisdom, ever mindful of the perfection you seek.

79 Remember the laws of health and vitality and live them well that your body might always be well, even into your ancient age.

80 Be moderate and temperate in all things, but also passionate in the joys of your righteous pleasures.

81 Ever seek to develop and maintain a perfect physique for your age, with health and strength and stamina that belies your years.

82 Never be satisfied with where you are, for when you stop reaching, you do not remain where you are, but slide backward to become less than you were.

83 Cultivate the garden of your mind. Nourish the flowers within, that your garden may always remain vibrant, but also plant new flowers of knowledge each day that your garden may ever be growing and expanding, even until it holds flowers from all the world.

84 Be noble and pure in your thoughts. Purge your mind of pettiness, greed, vanity, jealousy, craving, and hurtful ambition.

85 Cultivate divine thoughts and sentiments. See the good in people and situations, and you will bring it out in them and in yourself.

86 Think not so much of what you can do for yourself, but more of what you can do for others.

87 Consider how you can be a light of benefit, happiness and help to others, especially to your family and those you love with a sacred love.

88 Let not your mind think along dark and crooked paths, but seek out the straight and narrow, illuminated

by the brilliant light of virtue.

89 It is the weak man who gives up the light of his mind and turns it to darkness, becoming crude in language and actions, cunning, sly, manipulative, secretive, a hidden danger to all who know him.

90 Seek instead examples of greatness and light and emulate them. Be idealistic in your character and ever strive to reach your ideals.

91 Look at other men and women who have achieved at least a part of that which you seek, who have obtained the pinnacle of a mountain of character you desire to embody.

92 Consider how you can be like unto them, for surely as one man has become, so may others be; for in every light that you see, so too can you shine.

93 And if you thus endeavor for perfection in your life, not as a zealot, but in harmony, peace, forbearance, and love, then you shall find the bliss that you seek, the harmony of oneness, and the precious bond to the love of our divine Mother and Father that is the balm to all pains and the river to transcendent joy.

94 Even if you never reach the ideal you seek, be not discouraged, for if you strive faithfully, you will become the embodiment of the character which you sought.

95 Therefore, in your pursuit of sweet perfection, do not be a perfectionist or berate yourself for falling short, for perfection is not for this life but the next, and if you are seeking your goals with honest effort, you are achieving them even while you seek.

96 Verily, if you strive with sincerity and purpose to embody a divine character and never abandon your

sweet spirit or idealism, you are a success in your endeavors of eternal significance, every day of your life.

97 Is it little wonder that even in a society of darkness that the man or woman who embodies such an ethical and moral character becomes a priceless jewel, a firm, reliable tower of light from which even those in darkness take comfort?

98 When you are challenged by mortal life, as you always shall be, let this be a time when the true divinity of your character comes forth. Do not allow times of stress and turmoil to shake you from your foundation.

99 And what is your foundation? You are a child of God, a Child of Light, literally a priceless son or daughter of divinity. Even through the fog of mortal upheavals and the tumults and tribulations, always remember you are still a child of God and shall inherit joy and kingdoms beyond measure, as you remain true to your light.

100 Elohim the Father and the Mother are the source of all things that exist, and you are a part of the source and they are a part of you. Even when the agitation and anxieties of life cloud your memory, it does not change the truth: You are a child of God, a Child of Light, a priceless son or daughter of divinity.

101 You are founded upon Celestine Light. You live, move, and have your soul filled with the divine light, whether you know it or not.

102 Everything that exists, that has existed, or that will exist, both the living and the inanimate, were created through the Celestine Light of Elohim. That divine light remains within them, a part of them, throughout all

eternity.

103 Because the divine light of Elohim exists within all things from their creation, so Elohim remains in all things and all people. Elohim is all-pervading. By the word of Elohim countless Earths and the stars that surround them were created, and the Celestine Light of Elohim is inseparable from them.

104 Though people and places may become shrouded in darkness, there will always remain at least a sliver of the light. And from that sliver, the light may always grow, even until it overcomes the darkness.

105 Therefore, remember, remember, when you are of weak faith or downtrodden by the torments of mortality, that you are ever a child of God whether you remember it or not, that within you waiting always to see the light is a divine perfection, a divine bliss, a divine love for the sacred and the holy.

106 When men do evil, they cover the light of their divine nature and hide it from themselves and others. The more evil they do, the more the light is hidden.

107 But never forget that no matter how evil a man becomes, he can never eradicate the divine light of Elohim that is inescapably a part of his soul forever.

108 And the same divine light of the soul that calls man to his greatness will also condemn the man who heeds not the calling and instead does evil in his life.

109 For after mortality, there will come a day of judgment, and it will be the divine light of his own soul that judges the man, when he looks into the light and sees his shadow.

110 If his light has been hidden by his evil acts, it will

shine but a glimmer of its former glory and great will be his shadow. But if he has fulfilled his destiny, the light of his soul will be brilliant; radiating forth in every direction, even so much that there will be no shadow.

111 Thus, man is judged not by the Elohim, but by his own soul, by his light and his shadow, which shows without prejudice or favor how well he fulfilled his own destiny of divinity in mortality.

112 Now you live upon a tumultuous Earth. Disease, famine, pestilence, and war may overcome you at any time. If you live in the light of Elohim, you will be prepared, and through all these challenges, you will more likely stand, even while others fall.

113 Nevertheless, if your sojourn in mortality ends before you have been able to strive in fullness for your perfection, you have no cause to mourn, for your opportunity has not ended, nor can it ever end, for there is no end to your radiant, eternal spirit, and soul.

114 Remember, you are not the frail mortal shell which you see in the mirror, but a radiant, immortal child of divinity, which weapons cannot kill, fire cannot burn, disease cannot wrack, and sadness cannot overwhelm.

115 You were not born, nor can you die. You are eternal, permanent, beyond time, and death has no meaning for you. You are everlasting, immortal, indestructible, deathless, and without birth, save the birth of your spirit and soul through the love of your Heavenly Father and Mother before this world was.

116 Whatever tragedies, afflictions, or sorrows occur in your life, even unto death, happen not to you, but only upon your shell of mortality, the frail covering of

flesh and bones housing your soul.

117 This oh-so-temporary shell does not need a pestilence or disease or war to destroy it. When it becomes old, if it survives the wars and pestilences and diseases, it will still wear out and cease to be.

118 Therefore, be not so concerned about the number of years given to your mortal shell, for there are a myriad of ways by which it can come to an end—some sooner, others later—but to an end it shall always come.

119 Be more concerned with your indestructible and immortal soul and what you can do in the years given unto you in mortality to perfect it and help it to radiate its glory. This is your destiny.

120 And if through accident or disease or war or tribulation, your sojourn in mortality ends before its time, you shall be given another, even until you have had ample opportunity to fulfill the full measure of your mortal experience.

121 Like unto the schoolhouse in your town burning down, the destruction of your mortal shell, if premature, does not end the opportunity for your soul to expand in mortality; for even as another school would be built in your town that you could continue your education, so shall another mortal shell be given unto your soul in another mortal life, perhaps even on another Earth, that you might have the opportunity to fulfill the full measure of your mortality.

122 I say again, fear not the frailties of mortality, even unto death. Even were all life upon your Earth to be destroyed by the follies of man, you remain, you are not touched, you are not destroyed, for you are sons and

daughters of God and you are as eternal as the Elohim.

123 Your destiny remains true and clear; you are not the body, but the soul. Your soul is you, and you are eternal.

124 You are light; you are good; you are one with all of creation.

125 Therefore, ever seek to fulfill the divinity of your creation, ever doing good, ever welcoming the resonance of the spirit of Elohim into the bosom of your soul, ever seeking the perfection of your being in every way. This is your destiny."

SERMON IN NAZARETH

Excerpted from Oracles of Celestine Light, Nexus: Chapter 21

On Yeshua's last day in Nazareth, before he and Miriam began their journey to Bethany, his family and kinsfolk and the people of Nazareth, realizing that Yeshua was leaving perhaps never to return, asked him to give them some words of wisdom before he departed.

2 Even those that had always looked down upon him as strange and peculiar asked him to speak, for they knew despite their disdain that he held knowledge few men had.

3 Thus, it was that nearly all the people of Nazareth came to the little hill outside of town where Yeshua had taught his family the Contemplative Meditation Movements. And they sat upon the gentle slope and gazed upward at Yeshua standing atop the rise that all might see and hear his voice.

4 And Yeshua said unto them, "Hear the thanks of my heart to you, my family and friends, and neighbors of Nazareth. It is here among you that I have been sheltered and nurtured and learned much of life and truth. Wherever I go in the days to come, you will always be with me in my heart, and God will always look with favor upon you for the kindnesses you have

given unto me and my wife and my children.

5 "I know not where to begin, therefore let one of you stand and ask of me the questions of your mind and the troubles of your heart, and from that, I will give unto you a fullness of my knowledge as God has given me the substance for which was asked."

6 Then to the surprise of many, before a man could stand, Shavna, the widow, stood and quickly said to him, "I have been a widow for three years. My only son was crucified by the Romans the year before last and my parents are dead. I still have three children in the tiny hovel of my home and barely exist upon baskets that I make for a merchant and the little that my brother, who is here with me and himself infirmed, can give me.

7 "According to the law, I must be double veiled and cloaked to be outside, so that even now I can scarcely see you or breathe. Why is life so hard and especially why does God allow women to be treated barely above the animals? Even to speak to you as I now am shall bring condemnation upon me."

8 Yeshua was very moved by her words and said unto all the multitude. "Hear me, O Children of Israel. This woman's words cause anguish to my soul."

9 And he asked for Miriam, his wife, to come and stand with him on the hill. And she alone, among all the women of Nazareth, was not cloaked or veiled.

10 And Yeshua said unto the multitude, "This is Miriam, my beloved wife, and you see the fairness of her face as fully as I do. And it is I that have asked her not to hide the beauty of the face God has given. For what God has given is not for man to take away.

11 She is not a harlot, but a most virtuous and pleasing daughter of God, a delight to Elohim in her every word and deed.

12 Verily, the wicked lusts of men are not her sin but theirs, for she does not look to them or entice them, and any who lusts upon her shall be held accountable for every impure thought on the Judgment Day.

13 And more, she sits beside me at councils and in all things do I consider her opinion, and many have been the wise words she has given unto me.

14 I say unto you that it is man that is too often the abomination unto God and women in their virtue who God favors, for it is man that makes war and man that enslaves and man that rapes and man that despoils and man that murders and man that does all manner of evil in the world.

15 But of all the sins men do, the trampling of women underfoot, even their very wives and daughters, is among the most loathsome sins unto God.

16 "If Miriam was to stand here naked before you and innocent of all offense or outward temptation, whose sin would it be? Verily, it could not be her sin for she was merely being as God had made her, but it would be the sin of every man who lusted upon her and the sin of every man or woman who judged her in her nakedness.

17 Therefore, I say unto you, ask not women to cloak and veil themselves, if it is not their desire; for the crown of their temple is their eyes and their face and their hair, which is beautiful as God has made, and to see this wonder in purity and respect is to honor the maker.

18 Ask instead to have control over the evil inside of

you to not imagine perverted thoughts of the temple God has built. For I say unto you that on the Day of Judgment, man shall be weighed in the balance by every impure thought as well as act.

19 And to the men, I say again, seek not to be masters over your women, especially not to the point of servitude and degradation, but seek rather to be master of the carnal man within you who lusts after the virtuous and sins against the righteous.

20 And to the women I say, fear not to show your face, for it is a glory of God, but be modest in your dress and look not at men to entice, nor to allure them by sensual speaking, for then the fault is yours for the evil you stir in the hearts of men; and then it is both you and the man that shall be accountable on the Day of Judgment.

21 Let all remember as Solomon has said, 'He that conquers himself is greater than he that takes a city.' Therefore, I say unto you, be masters of yourselves.

22 There once was a hermit who was so afraid to sin that he left his family and built a one-room house without windows outside of the city walls so that he would not see anything that would tempt him to sin. He never came out except once each week, clothed in a robe with a deep cowl, to go to a market on the outskirts of the city to sell the trinkets he made and buy a little food.

23 And so he passed his life until the day when he was an old man, and a great storm came from the desert and knocked down his little house and blew away his possessions and left him standing in the brightness of the sun with only the clothes on his back.

24 The man was forced to go into the city to seek food and shelter, and he passed much devastation, for many had been afflicted by the storm.

25 Then came a well-dressed man through the streets with many people following him. And spying the hermit, he asked him to come with him and told him that he would give him shelter and food. So the hermit went with the man.

26 As they passed through the streets, the well-dressed man called others who had misfortune to him, promising shelter and food. And many people followed the man as he climbed a hill at the center of the city, until at last they came upon a large white house at the top where lived their benefactor, the richest merchant in all the city.

27 He brought the people into his home and gave of them everything he had: all of his food, all of his fine clothes, and the space anywhere in his house they desired to walk or to make a bed. And despite his fears, the hermit found he had no coveting thoughts, but only gratitude.

28 And the hermit found that though he was looking at the men and women, some with their garments in great disarray, that despite his fears, he was finding no wicked or lustful thoughts toward them, but only sympathy for sharing the same misfortune as he.

29 Then the hermit walked onto a balcony, overlooking the azure blue sea, a sight he had not looked upon since his youth, and despite his fears, he had no thoughts to irresponsibly sail away with the first ship, but instead was content to remain where he was and instead gave

thought to how that which had been destroyed might be rebuilt.

30 As he viewed the city below him and all of the grand buildings of stone which he had never seen, he wondered what they could be. And despite his fears of the past, he did not feel compelled to do evil simply because he knew there would be evil somewhere in the city below.

31 The following day, with a belly full of good food and a fine new robe from his benefactor, the hermit walked down into the city to explore all he had never seen. Throughout the day, he was like unto a little child, overjoyed with each new surprise, but innocent in his wonder, and never once tempted to sin though there were temptations at every turn.

32 As the night began to fall, he returned to the house of the rich man where a great meal had been prepared for all of the guests. Even though everyone had just experienced devastation from the storm, all was forgotten in the comforts and good company of the rich man's house.

33 The following day, the rich man came to all of his guests and asked them where they had lived and what type of house they had lived in. He told them he was going to rebuild their houses, every one, even if he needed to sell his grand house to afford his gift to those in need, for as God had blessed him, he had covenanted to bless others.

34 When he came to ask the hermit what type of house he had lived in so that he might plan for rebuilding it, the hermit was ashamed to tell him and therefore just

told him it was a small house on the outside of the city, but did not tell him it had been built without windows.

35 That night as he lay in a comfortable place, he was not comfortable inside his skin and could not sleep, for he was tormented by the realization that he had seen so many men and so many women and so many wonders of the city and never once had he sinned or been tempted to sin.

36 He thought of the rich man who was giving all that he had to help those in need and realized that in his life, he had only thought to help himself, and even in that, he had only given himself to emptiness. And he wept in the memory of all the years of his life he had lost and the relationships he had spurned and, unlike the rich man, all the good he had never done for his family and fellow man.

37 All of his isolation would have been worth it, he reasoned, if it had been the only way to keep him from sin, as he had supposed. But in now seeing everything he had seen and not having been tempted to sin, he came to understand that his sins of youth were not because of other people or the simple life of the city, but because of his own weaknesses of the flesh and spirit.

38 Now he understood that his weaknesses could be overcome by changing his thoughts, for as his thoughts became pure and full of kindness and charity, so too did his actions. And what was weak had become strong.

39 Upon the morning, he went to the rich man and told him he had once been a builder and asked if he could now be a servant in his house that he might help him in helping others, as he was wont to do.

40 The rich man was overjoyed that he had a heart to give aid to his fellow man, but would not have him be a servant. Instead, he asked that the hermit would help his neighbors in their time of need and, in that service, would be serving him.

41 And so the hermit labored to help many people rebuild their homes. Then one day, his friends covered his eyes and brought him to the plot of ground where his house had stood before the storm. And opening his eyes, he discovered to his joy that in secret, they had rebuilt a new house for him with three rooms and windows for air and light upon every wall.

42 Thereafter, the hermit spent his days, tending the gardens of his neighbors and became known through all the city for his kindness of spirit and helpfulness to others.

43 He spent his last years building a grand fountain, stone by stone, and asked his rich friend to run water to it. When he died, many turned out to bid him good-bye, and for many years, the Hermit's Fountain remained outside the city gates, next to the empty house with windows on every wall, kept clean and tidy by all of his friends to welcome and give relief to the weary travelers coming from the desert.

44 And I say unto the men among you that you have the choice in your life to be like the hermit who was conquered by the fear of sin and a slave to his fears, becoming a shell of a man to whom friends did not exist and neighbors were unknown.

45 Or like the hermit who conquered the temptations of sin to become the master of himself, flying free in his

soul, a joy to his neighbors, a delight to his friends, and a light unto the world.

46 Remember, O people of Nazareth, as you sow, so shall you reap, both in Heaven and on earth, for as you confine the righteous spirits of others or bind their worthy lives into emptiness, you also become a shell of what you could have been and exist in a world inside your soul as confining to your spirit as the hermit's house with no windows.

47 Or you may draw the favor of God and man and choose to be like the rich man who judged not the lowly state of his brothers and sisters from the children of Elohim, but gave unto them all that he had in their hour of need and this without condition, but only with love. Unto such as this, God will say at the Judgment Day, 'Well done, my good and faithful servant.'

48 If I must part from you my family and friends and neighbors of Nazareth, let me part with these words: That you remember you are all sons and daughters of God, and therefore, you are all brothers and sisters in the spirit of God.

49 And I tell you in all truth that men and women are equal before God in their creation. But in the judgment, it will always be found that there have been more virtuous women than righteous men.

50 Therefore, men, I say unto you, be faithful to your wives in thought and deed. Honor and respect your wives and your daughters for their virtue and abilities. Think not to place them below you, but hold them beside you that all may go forward together to a greater light. And do not demand that they be cloaked

into invisibility because of the impure thoughts of a few sinful men.

51 And to the women I say, honor and respect your husbands. Do not hide your glory which Elohim has made in your beauty, but be modest in your manner and dress that your husbands need not worry about the impure thoughts of unrighteous men toward those they love, that your moments together may always be comforting and joyous.

52 Unto all I say, look to and care for one another. Be as the rich man. Even if you are poor, be rich in your spirit and in your desire to do good. Suffer there not to be any among you in agony of spirit because their cupboard is bare or their roof lets in the rain or with a spirit that is broken because of foul deeds done to them.

53 By this, you may know a true man of God: that he honors the temple of his body both inside and out; that he is humble and has humor and laughter and smiles, despite the adversities of life; that he honestly keeps the commandments of Sinai; that he plays with his children and provides for their needs; that he is of service to his community without reward or acclaim; and that he loves and respects his wife and ever encourages and supports her and helps her to expand her light and have joy.

54 And by this, you may know a true woman of God: that she honors the temple of her body inside and out; that she is not vain; that she smiles and laughs easily and greets her husband with warmth and care; that she keeps the commandments of Sinai; that she makes her home a piece of Heaven, no matter how humble it may be; that it is always a refuge of peace and comfort for

her husband and her children; that she plays with her children and sees to their education and welfare; that she is of service to her sisters in need as she can be; and that she loves and respects her husband and ever encourages and supports him and helps him to expand his light and have joy.

55 You have been accustomed to think of yourselves as separate families living within the town of Nazareth. May you begin to consider yourselves as the family of Nazareth, living within the Celestine Light of Elohim.

56 As one undivided, the happiness and comfort of all is magnified. As one undivided, the trials and tribulations of life are eased. As one undivided, you will live long upon the land and prosper, despite the Romans and all else the world may do. My brothers and sisters of light, make it so."

57 And Yeshua continued to hear the questions of the people of Nazareth and give answers unto them that lifted their spirits and filled their souls. And all of the other words that Yeshua spoke that day are written in the Book of Yakov, given to the Children of Light in Jerusalem.

TRUTH OF A PROPHET

Excerpted from Oracles of Celestine Light, Nexus: Chapter 23

Yeshua travels to the community of Gimron with Miriam's brother Lazarus to visit Yochanan where they spend eight days, during which time Yeshua gives a sermon on how to know a true prophet of God.

While Yeshua had been away from Gimron, Yochanan had grown in stature spiritually as well as physically, and many in the community now looked to him for guidance and inspiration because of his fervor and conviction.

11 Thus, it was on the following day, there were
sermons being given by the high priests, and Yochanan
and Yeshua and Lazarus were invited to attend and
listen. Yochanan, though still unmarried, was asked to
speak at the end of the meeting to rouse their spirits.
12 And it came to pass that the high priests spoke on
the calling of a prophet and how the penalty of Moses
for a false prophet was death by stoning. And there were
lamentations from many in the room about the many
false prophets wandering the land of Israel, leading
good people astray and away from the purity of the
principles of God.
13 One of the men present, named Tomas, exclaimed,

"I have heard some called prophets in Jerusalem, and each sounds as good as the other, but they proclaim different teachings. How then are we to know which one to stone and which one to heed? For God will surely condemn us if we put to death a man whom he had called and will not forgive our error or ignorance."

14 After much debate upon this subject, Yochanan was asked to say the final words. And Yochanan rose and said unto them, "My esteemed brethren and Elders, I know that God chooses whom he will to reveal his secrets and desires unto the children of men, and it is not for men or priests or governments to judge the prophets God has called or the truths that they reveal; nevertheless, they do.

15 "And among the Children of Israel, it would seem that to know a true prophet is very simple, for as the priests tell us, either a prophet teaches the Law of Moses or he does not, and by this you may know them.

16 But though I am young, I have learned that blindly following the law does not always lead to the light. I have learned that if we would know pure truth, we must not obey without question the persuasions of men or the authority of the priests, but each of us must ask God to reveal the truth unto us and trust that the spirit of Elohim will let our hearts understand things our minds cannot know.

17 If your own discernment is lacking, which I think all of us would agree is sometimes the case, then I say it is good to consider the discernment of those whom you respect in these matters for their wisdom and fairness; those whom you know accept not the dictates of men,

but weigh each matter with God.

18 And in this, I know there are some who look to me, and I am greatly humbled by such an honor, especially in consideration of my young age and inexperience with life.

19 But upon the foundation of such worth that men may esteem me, I would like to give my place to Yeshua bar Yosef of Nazareth whom I testify has been called of God; whom I testify speaks the words of God. This I know to be true. With every breath of my body, this I know to be true."

20 Then Yochanan sat down abruptly and amid an exquisite silence Yeshua rose among them and said unto them, "Men are only led astray by false prophets because of the vanities of their hearts and the delusions of their minds.

21 Of vanity, man must repent and forsake, and of delusions, man must do all he can to reason the truth in his mind and then humble himself before God and ask for the Holy Spirit to give a sure knowing of the truth in his heart.

22 And unto the righteous, the Holy Spirit of Elohim will always speak in a still small voice in his mind and a warm contentedness in his heart that all men of virtue may know truth from falsehood.

23 But the man seduced by the world, in his vanity, in his desire for comfort and ease, in his desire to indulge his sins and wanton ways, in his desire to keep authority over his fellow men, becomes deaf and dulled to the promptings of God.

24 Though he may inquire still of God in his times

of need, his ears will hear only the deafening sound of silence, for Elohim does not speak even in the smallest of voices to the man who mocks God by the manner of his life.

25 Thus, man is left standing alone, with a part of him seduced to the ways of the world and a part of him still longing for the sweetness of God, and he is wracked with torment inside, not knowing the way to turn.

26 Verily, I say unto you the ways of God are easy to know and that no man may ever be deceived; take now the lamp that I bring, whereby in its light, you may see and discern truth from error when men say they speak from God.

27 Many have said that the Law of Moses clearly tells how the people may know a true prophet from a false; therefore why do we speak of these things?

28 But I ask, do you worship a dead or a living God? For if all you have for your faith and the actions of your life are the laws of ancient times, then you have only a part of what God has given for the good of man.

29 Some say a true prophet will never speak anything that is contrary to what has been given in the law, saying the law came from God; therefore, anything that is different cannot be of God.

30 Think you that the world never changes? That never is there a need for greater light to illuminate the darkness of a world far different than the one in which the ancient prophets lived?

31 Think you that the children of men never become better than their ancestors and worthy of greater light?

32 And I say unto you that if the words of God to

men were meant to never be added upon, then you would not need the writings of many ancient prophets to say these words, but the writings of only one, for God would have spoken just once, unto a single prophet, to reveal all that man would ever need.

33 But God continued to speak from prophet to prophet because man continued to need new light and additional knowledge and guidance for the challenges of his times.

34 Even as the prophet Amos has said, "Surely the Lord God will do nothing, but that he first reveals his secrets unto his servants, the prophets."

35 And I say unto you that the Almighty Elohim, the creator of Heaven and earth, is not a god who does nothing, but the God to which nothing is impossible. And by the mouths of his holy prophets, his will is made known unto men.

36 In the days to come, there will walk upon the earth children of men worthy of a far-greater light than has even been given to you or to Moses or to Abraham. And unto them will Elohim bless with greater and glorious understanding.

37 From my lips, you will hear words you have never heard, for I do not repeat the dusty laws of the past you memorized long ago, but give unto you greater light and knowledge, even as the prophets of old each gave greater light and knowledge to the Children of Israel who walked with them.

38 Many of the ancient laws in the sacred texts were given only for that people, in that time, concerning their lives and their challenges, which were unique to them.

39 Thus, does God always bless those who strive for the light so that as they live worthy, they will always have a prophet in their midst to guide them through the perils of their day.

40 Nevertheless, Elohim has also given sacred laws that are not just for that time, but are eternal and inviolate, meant to be lived by all men, for all time, such as the commandments of Sinai.

41 How then can men know which laws of the prophets of old are meant for all time and which are only meant for a season of time? How can men know if a prophet today utters true words from God or false words to deceive?

42 I say unto you that laws that are meant for all men in all times are laws that have eternal significance, both on earth and in Heaven.

43 The eternal paths of God are scarcely concerned with the temporal ways of man, save that man keeps the commandments of Sinai and respects the temple of his body, which God has made, both on the inside and the outside, and this that he might live long upon the land and have many years to do good and prove that he honors God by honoring the temple God has given him.

44 Therefore, it matters not to God how many steps one takes on the Sabbath or other such pious dictates from the dusty past, for what has this to do with things of forever?

45 Man is upon the earth to learn to draw near to the light and to flee from the darkness; to prove by his life that he follows Elohim and the goodness thereof, by

striving each day to cleave to the light; to be a better husband and father and brother and do good to all men.

46 You have heard it said that man is made in the image of God. Think you that these hallowed words speak only of the way man appears? I say unto you, nay. The image of God means as well all the attributes of Elohim.

47 It is given to man in this life to emulate God and to show by his life how greatly he desires to be like him.

48 You are wise to be wary because of false prophets, for there are many that come to men in the name of God clothed as meek sheep, but inside are ravenous wolves.

49 Therefore, when a man comes forth proclaimed by himself or others to be a prophet of God, see that you test the teachings that he says, not in how they call men to the letter of the law or to some strange doctrine, but whether they cause men to do good to their fellow men and to take righteous and pure actions or entice them into darkness or constrain their spirit with the needless dictates of men, especially those given by man but proclaimed to be of God.

50 And see that you test the man that his life fulfills the good teachings he proclaims, for though Elohim may call a sinner who has repented to be a prophet, he will not give his light to any who remain in darkness by their words or deeds.

51 Look therefore to the simple examples Elohim has given for all men to see. Do men gather grapes of thorns or figs of thistles? Even so, every good tree brings forth good fruit and only good fruit; even as a true prophet of God calls upon man to do good and only good in ways

that expand his spirit, not shut it in a box.
52 When men find a tree that brings forth bad fruit, they hew it down and burn it in the fire, for it is worthless unto them, and left in place only is a hindrance to the good that might grow in the soil.
53 Wherefore, I say unto you, of true prophets, by their fruits, you shall know them."
54 And many were amazed at the words of Yeshua, and for some, the impact on their heart was powerful and it changed them from that moment. But others were very wroth at him and considered him a false prophet who ridiculed the law upon which all prophets must stand and blasphemed the true concepts of God.

FIRST SERMON IN BETHANY

Excerpted from the Oracles of Celestine Light, Nexus: Chapter 24

Yeshua and Miriam spent two more days in
Bethany and after the evening meal on the last
night, Miriam's family and kinsfolk gathered
to hear Yeshua speak, for many had heard stories of his
teachings in Nazareth, and some thought he might be
a Prophet.
2 And Yeshua said unto them, "There are those that
say the Kingdom of God is outside of you; that it is in
the sky and in the sea and in the temple built by man
of great stones and precious woods. But I say unto you,
that the greater Kingdom is inside of you, for you are
the temple of light, built by God.
3 When you come to know yourselves in purity,
forgetting the conceptions of the world and the
teachings of men, then you will realize that you are true
sons and daughters of the living Father and Mother in
Heaven and are inheritors of all that your parents have,
as you live worthy to receive your inheritance.
4 In ignorance, some will say it is blasphemy to speak
of God in the plural, as a male and a female, a husband
and a wife co-creating; to them I say, have you not heard
of the creation of the world where it is written in the
sacred scrolls, let us make man in our image, after our

likeness; and of when man was cast out of the garden God said, behold, the man has become as one of us; and of when God confounded the languages at Babel and said, let us go down and confound their language?

5 The sacred texts teach that man was made in the image of God. How then do men claim that God is only a male, for does not the body of a man differ greatly from the body of a woman? Therefore, I say unto you, man is made in the image of the Father and woman is made in the image of the Mother.

6 In fullness, a man is not without woman, nor husband without wife, neither parents without a child. And the perfection of God is the Father and the Mother and the Son; three lights each to their own, but they are one God, united in perfect spirit, understanding and purpose.

7 Did not Isaiah see the parents speaking of the coming of the Son unto the children of men and of the rejection of the truth thereof? For it is written, I heard the voice of the Lord, saying, whom shall I send and who will go for us?

8 Then said I, here I am, send me.

9 And he said, Go and tell this to the people: hear you indeed, but understand not; and see you indeed but perceive not.

10 The hearts of this people are fat; they make their ears heavy and shut their eyes; lest they hear with their ears and see with their eyes, and understand with their hearts, and convert, and be healed.

11 Again Isaiah spoke of the Father that is Lord, and of the Mother, the spirit that touches the hearts of men,

and of the Son, who redeems the righteous, for it is written, from the beginning, from the time that it was, there am I: and now the Lord God and his spirit has sent me."

12 And Yeshua said unto them, "He who has ears to hear and eyes to see; let him hear and see."

13 Then Levi son of Phinehas, who had studied the law, said, "I have eyes and ears but I have not seen or heard of the God you describe taught in the sacred scrolls. If God is three divine individuals acting as one, and not one divine essence, then why is this not more plain? For there are thousands of places in the sacred scrolls that refer to God as one force, which is personalized in a masculine way, and only these few you have given to the contrary that may merely be errors of transcribing. What more can you say about this vital subject?"

14 Yeshua answered him, saying, "Even among the honest of heart, it is the nature of man to see and hear that which he wishes to see and hear; and to the contrary, he is blind and deaf. How many times have you held the answer to your question in your hand, but have not seen the truth because you were not seeking it? Read again that which you have read, and look for the gems that speak of the plurality of God, and you shall find that which you seek.

15 Verily I say unto you, Elohim is the name for God, and as used in the sacred books it is a word of both male and female nature and reflects the plural, not the individual; and of it, the holy scrolls speak thousands of times. Verily, it is the Father and the Mother, and through the Son they do all things."

16 Then Yeshua took a stick and wrote the letters YHVH on the ground and said unto them, "This is the sacred name of the Father, given unto the children of men; which name should not be spoken, but only written in reverence, and never defaced.

17 Before the world was, the Elohim decided that which each of them should do to bring to pass the eternal progression and exaltation of the spirit children of the Father and the Mother.

18 The Son said he would do whatsoever the Father and the Mother asked of him, and that through him their will would be manifested among the children of men.

19 The Mother said she would be the spirit of Elohim that would reside within the hearts of every child upon the earth, and stay with them for all of their days as they kept their temple worthy to have her, and sincerely lived for truth and righteousness.

20 The Father said he would connect to every particle of existence that he might ever receive the supplications of the children of men that the Elohim could bless the righteous.

21 Therefore, the Children of Light should pray to the Father and the Mother, who are one and over all; and ask in the name of the Son, through whom all good things occur, that they may be touched in wisdom and richly blessed, as they seek righteousness in harmony with the will of Elohim. And the humble shall be comforted with heavenly love by the Mother, who sends forth the Holy Spirit of Elohim to manifest sweet blessings unto the Children of Light.

22 Among the Children of Israel this is not understood, but it is now known unto you.

23 When you have a goodly need, and are humble and not proud, seek out God by calling on Elohim; for even as the word leaves your lips the love and attention of the Father and the Mother and the Son comes upon you in fullness and power."

24 Then said Levi, "How strange a doctrine you teach, but you speak as one with authority, therefore I will study upon the things you have said. But tell me this, for it is a mystery to me; if we are to ask of the Father in the name of the Son, what then is the name of the Son?

25 Yeshua answered unto him, saying, "Look again in the sacred scriptures and you will find it there as it was spoken by your fathers; but verily I say unto you, that in your life, you will live to hear the name of the Son as it is known among the children of men, spoken on the lips of many people, some with great anger and some with great love."

26 Then Gideon, a cousin of Miriam, asked, "Speak to us of marriage and Heaven, for in our family it is a tangled web; we have marriages that have come after marriages, some with a man and a widow and some with a man married to several wives, some whom are widows. I have heard conflicting things from different Rabbis regarding this matter. What has God said to you of this?"

27 And Yeshua said unto them, "When you marry, you have heard it said that at death the marriage is ended, be it a marriage of one man and one woman or one man and several women; and so it is for the marriages

sanctified by man, for they have no force in Heaven.

28 But I say unto you that if it is by God, with the man and the woman having asked together for the blessings of Elohim; and sealed with vows between them for it to be a sacred and eternal covenant, and this before the witness of family and friends; then it is not parted at death, but with the righteous, remains in force for time and all eternity, as long as both the man and the woman live worthy of the blessing.

29 In the hereafter, everyone will have eternal life and come forth to their just and resonate reward, be it joyous or despairing, according to their faith in God and the paths they choose in life. But even among the most righteous, man cannot be without woman or woman without man if they desire to go forward into the greatest exaltation.

30 But if a marriage is by the authority of man, or the rituals of men, or the governments of men, or the priesthoods of men, then it ends with death; for in the eternity God is not bound by the ordinances of man which have no power to bind in Heaven; they become as dust and are trampled under feet in the world to come.

31 Nor can marriage be performed in Heaven, for it is an ordinance given to be fulfilled in the flesh, that it may be proven that the man will faithfully cleave unto the woman and the woman unto the man, despite all that evil may tempt.

32 In fidelity to their marriage they magnify the gift of life God has given, and shall therefore have so much more reward in the world to come.

33 But whosoever is married only by the authority of

man, or of governments, or the priesthoods of men, shall
not be married in Heaven, until their love is fulfilled by
a resonant proxy of two in the flesh.
34 Moreover, know that as a man is not without a
woman, nor woman without a man, neither can either
stand before Elohim without the other, for alone they
are but half of a whole, and only in the wholeness and
balance of love and commitment can the Celestine
Light of God be fully manifested."
35 Then Gideon said, "But what of those who may
love true, but pass from life unknowing of the way to
secure their relationship for eternity?"
36 And Yeshua said unto him, "The covenant that
binds for eternity is forged in the love that endures and
grows stronger through all the trials of life because it is
lit by the Celestine Light of Elohim and the unselfish
oneness of two. It is a beautiful flower nurtured with
exceeding tenderness and consideration that upon life's
passing is most brilliant.
37 Every day of life together is a witness to the world
of their devotion to God and to each other. Such a love,
after many years together to prove its truth, is dedicated
to continue in eternity by the holy desire of those
that love, and enshrined in the heart of Elohim from
everlasting to everlasting."
38 And Gideon replied, "But is there not an exact way
in which holy ordinances should be performed?"
39 Yeshua answered him, saying, "With man, the
letter of the law is so important, but with God it is the
conviction of the heart, the righteousness of the life,
and worthy desires of the soul that matters.

40 And Yeshua, perceiving that some were confused by that which he spoke said, "Verily, if you will not listen to your heart, which speaks the truth your customary mind does not know, then you do not know yourselves, and you will dwell in poverty, and it is you who are that poverty, no matter the riches of the world which you may possess."

41 And the people were amazed for never before had they heard such teachings.

42 Yeshua continued, saying, "Recognize what is in your sight, and the feeling that is in your heart. Pray to your Father and Mother in Heaven for the light of understanding to expand into the testimony of truth, and then that which is hidden from you will become plain to you, and there is nothing hidden which will not become illuminated by the Celestine Light of Elohim."

43 They understood that he spoke of his teachings, but only a few understood that he also spoke of himself; and some people nodded in agreement but others shook their heads in disbelief.

44 And Yeshua spoke again, saying, "If you bring forth the light which is within you, what you bring forth will save you. If you do not bring forth the light within you, if you allow yourself to be blinded by the darkness of the world and the teachings of men, then what you do not bring forth will condemn you at the last day."

45 Perceiving from their mumblings that some among his listeners were concerned with following the dictates of the law and their appearances before men, and desired to not quietly find the light within themselves, he said, "Why do you wash the outside of the temple but

the inside leave dirty?

46 If it is pleasing for the outside to be clean, which is only seen by men, how much more pleasing is it for the inside to be clean, wherein resides that which nourishes you and is seen by God? Do you not realize that he who made the inside is the same one who made the outside?

47 If you would find favor with God, then be as concerned for the inside of your temple as for the outside, and let those that are high be like those that are low."

48 Then Nahor, son of Salathiel said, "All of these things you have said are strange doctrines that would seem to ridicule the law, and blasphemy the God of our fathers, and make women the equal of men."

49 Yeshua replied to him, saying, "The Celestine Light of the Kingdom is like a wise fisherman who one day was told by the king that he and all of the other fishermen of the village, could dive for pearls in the king's reserve and keep all that they found; but they must open each one before they gathered another so that none were wasted.

50 The other fishermen made haste to bring to shore and open as many oysters as they could harvest; and finding beds close to shore in shallow water, they soon had discovered a few small pearls; but the wise fisherman dove throughout the day in the deepest water, looking for the one large oyster that would have a pearl of great price; and he was ridiculed by his friends for the efforts he wasted in his faith.

51 As the sun began to set, many of the fishermen had small piles of pearls while the wise fisherman rose from the water again with nothing; and he was laughed at

again for his foolishness and faith.

52 But the wise fisherman's faith could not be shaken and with one last great breath he dove again to the deepest depth, and there he found an oyster of such size as men had never seen. And bringing it to the shore and opening it, he found the pearl of great price for his faith, and all the pearls of all of his friends put all together would not be a thousandth of the worth of his pearl.

53 Whoever has ears to hear, let him hear.

54 Verily, I say unto you, only when you look into your heart and find the child of God, only when you make the inside like the outside and the outside like the inside, only when those who are high are like those that are low, and only when you make the male and the female equal, so that they are two halves of one whole; only then will you have the light."

55 Hearing his words some were upset with his teachings and departed in anger, but more were amazed and delighted and held him in awe.

THE THREE BROTHERS

Excerpted from the Oracles of Celestine Light, Nexus: Chapter 33

While in Heliopolis, Yeshua spent much time, wandering the markets and the city and observing the Egyptians and their ways and the ways of the many visitors from other lands to be found within Heliopolis. And he asked many questions that he might have greater knowledge.

10 And it came to pass that one day as Yeshua was walking through the market that he saw a merchant crying in the back of his stall, and having compassion he went unto him and said, "Good sir, why do you weep?"

11 The merchant was ashamed to be seen with his emotions so openly, especially by a foreigner, and he replied, "I have not been weeping. I merely had some sand in my eye, which was hurting me, and I was trying to get it out."

12 And Yeshua said unto him, "As there seems to be nobody here for you to speak with at this time, and I am in need of a rest, do you mind if I sit for a moment in the shade and tell a story to you for the privilege?"

13 The merchant, seeing only an empty stall, assented to Yeshua's request. And Yeshua, knowing in his heart that he was despondent for the failure of his trading and in pain for his hungry children at home, whom he

loved, said unto him, "There once was a small caravan of three brothers that left Egypt to trade with the tribes in the desert.

14 Now the names of the three brothers were Strength, Righteous, and Perseverance."

15 Word spread quickly from one stall to another that a storyteller was in the marketplace, and as this was a cherished entertainment, people began to gather to hear the words of Yeshua.

16 And Yeshua said unto them, "Two elder brothers, Wisdom and Faithful, were left behind to care for the families, while their younger brothers sought to find success in trading, for all were in distress because of lack of money.

17 They traveled for three days, seeking to find tribes that encountered few traders that they might earn a good reward for their efforts.

18 On the third day, a great sandstorm came upon them, and they suffered under the wind and the stinging sands for a day and a night.

19 Not being familiar with the desert, they had been following the trail of camels that had passed before them. But now the storm had wiped away all traces of previous travelers, and in every direction, there was only barrenness.

20 The three brothers were despondent and could not decide which way to go. Even to return the way they had come was imperceptible to them.

21 And Righteous said unto his brethren, 'I should have remained at home to care for the families and let Wisdom come in my place, for he would know which

way to go.'

22 And Strength said unto his brethren, 'A little sandstorm is nothing! We still have seven days of water, and we are younger and better fit than Wisdom for a journey such as this. If we reason together, surely we can come upon the best way to go.'

23 And Perseverance said unto his brethren, 'We are squandering time as we speak. Come, let us choose which way to go and get on with it.'

24 And Righteous replied, 'You speak well, brothers, but let us place a marker here with our names and circumstances upon it, that any who may come upon it after us will know we have been here and were three days out of the city.'

25 Thus, it was that they decided to head into the sun as it was the one constant they thought they could rely upon. But this was not always easy as the terrain was hilly and they sometimes needed to change direction to get around obstacles, which put the sun at their side or at their backs.

26 Being from the city, where they lived among buildings, they had never paid much attention to the sun before. To their dismay, they noticed that it did not remain near the same spots of land as they thought it would, but moved vastly across the sky during the day, which caused great confusion as to the direction they should travel.

27 After seven days of suffering, they were sinking into the sand with exhaustion; their water was almost gone, and they had encountered no villages or any other travelers. They stopped upon a barren patch of sand, in

the empty desert of sand, and Strength and Righteous were ready to abandon hope and leave their bones upon that spot.

28 Only Perseverance still had hope and looked for a way of salvation. Then it was that he spied a few small plants that came only to his ankle, growing in a low spot between sand dunes. And he called to his brothers and said, 'Look here, brethren! Here is a plant; surely it must have water to survive. Therefore, let us dig here, and we will find our salvation.'

29 But his brothers were too fatigued to move, so Perseverance began to swiftly dig through the soft sand, first with his bare hands and then with a small pick, which they had brought with them, as the sand began to be packed and hard.

30 Soon he had a deep hole dug, but it was as dry inside of the hole as outside. Perseverance called unto his brothers saying, 'Come, help expand this opening for it makes a spot of shade, and beneath the level of the ground, it is cooler.'

31 Then his brothers came and with great slowness helped him to widen the hole so they all could fit inside. Perseverance pointed to the thread of a root from the plants that still continued deeper into the ground. And he said unto his brothers, 'Let us continue to dig deeper, for surely, this root must be going to water, or the plants would have withered in the sun. We owe it to our families to keep on trying to find life.'

32 Righteous was moved by his brother's words, and he began to help him dig. Resting often, they continued to dig until nightfall, until the hole was as deep as all

three brothers standing on top of one another, but still the sand was dry.

33 The next day, neither Righteous nor Strength could be persuaded to help Perseverance dig deeper, so while they lay still, he continued on his own.

34 After he had dug the depth of another man, his pick hit upon solid rock and he could go no further. In frustration, he threw the pick upon the stone and went back to his brothers to tell them.

35 And he said unto them, 'Even me, who never before has given up, must admit defeat. Let us bury ourselves in the hole we have dug, that our end will be quick and the desert can swallow us in our unworthiness, for we have left our families to destitution.'

36 And Strength was in sad agreement and, being the largest, stood to reach up and pull the sand upon them to bury them.

37 But Righteous reached for and held his arm to prevent the thing he would do, and he said unto them, 'Before we dishonor our families and take an action that cannot be undone, let us do the one thing that is yet left to us. We have sought salvation from ourselves alone, and life has rewarded us with misery. Let us now pray to the gods that they might intervene in our lives and save us.'

38 Strength and Perseverance agreed that nothing further could be lost by praying unto the gods, but amongst them they were uncertain as to which gods to pray to, and Righteous said unto them, 'Let us pray to the mightiest God, without a name. Let us just pray to the Almighty God.'

39 And it came to pass that the three brothers called out to the Almighty God and poured forth their hearts to him. In the greatest humility, they confessed their sins and promised to henceforth do only good with their lives. They beseeched him to save them, for the sake of their families.

40 They prayed all through the day to the Almighty God, and they began to feel a oneness with each other, and even with the desert and the grains of sand, such as they had never before felt or imagined. Then together they fell into a deep sleep.

41 Upon the sunrise, they awoke as one, and each had the same thought come alive in their head that the plant must still have water and that it must be beneath the rock.

42 Then Strength descended into the bottom of the hole and began to strike at the rock with mighty swings of the pick. But for all his efforts, there was nothing except a large hole in the rock.

43 But when at last his strength was failing and he thought he could swing no more, he determined to take one more mighty swing and as the pick hit upon the rock, it split asunder, and a geyser of water shot forth in such abundance that the brothers had to move quickly out of the hole to not be drowned.

44 And it came to pass that not only were the brothers saved, but they soon discovered the marker, which they had left only a short distance from the spring; and seeing a city in the distance, they discerned that in all their wanderings, they were not ten days away from their homes as they had assumed, but had circled

almost back to the beginning of their journey and were now close to the city from which they had left and to their wives and children.

45 Shortly thereafter, they moved their families and the families of their brothers, Wisdom and Faithful, to the spring they had discovered, and soon it blossomed into a garden of green and plenty that became a favored resting spot for the trading caravans.

46 And the brothers and their families prospered.

47 And from this story are many gems to enrich your life. Return to it again and again, and you will continue to find new treasures.

48 But the greatest treasure of all is to understand that there is an Almighty God in Heaven, and after all that man can do, there is still more that God will do for those who ask good things of them with a repentant heart and a humble spirit.

49 And I say unto you this day, look into your heart; reflect upon the journey of your soul in this life. Do not wait until you are dying in the desert to call upon the Almighty God; today is the day you are called unto repentance; today is the day you are called to humility; today is the day you are called to give yourself to God.

50 And whosoever hears my words and acts upon them shall know the true and living God, and they shall drink from the spring of everlasting water and never thirst again."

51 Then turning to the crowd that had gathered, Yeshua looked out among them all. And they had been captivated by his story and waited now for his next words. And he said unto them, "He who has ears

to hear, let him hear." Then he parted the crowd and walked away and returned to his family.

SANCTITY OF LIFE

Excerpted from the Oracles of Celestine Light, Nexus: Chapter 39

And it came to pass that a time of celebration occurred among the communities of the first cataract and a great feast was held, and many were the animals that were slaughtered to provide succor for the feast.

2 Yeshua and Miriam were invited to attend the festivities by the matriarch of the town in which they resided, and they did attend but ate no meat. This offended some of the men who had spent their efforts to gather the meat, and one of the warriors asked them, "How can you sit at our feast and dishonor us by not eating the food we have offered?"

3 And Yeshua said unto them, "We respect and honor the good desires of your heart to provide abundance to your people and your guests. But the animals you eat are our friends, and we could no more eat of their flesh than we could eat the flesh of one of our children.

4 And more than this is here, for these animals also had families and friends and children they loved, and when they died, their last moments were in pain and sorrow for those they love that were left behind, even their babies still suckling. No different than the sadness you would feel if an enemy killed you before your time.

Would not your last thoughts also be of those you loved that you would be with no more and of the tragedy of leaving them all alone?

5 Thus, the meat of the higher creatures that nurture their children and find happiness in their friends is tainted with the poison of unjust and untimely death, and any who eat of it take the poison of death into their body. And though they may be sustained that day, that which they eat takes away from the length of their days upon the earth.

6 And more than this, I say: Those who eat the flesh of the higher creatures take violence and killing into their heart and mind through the flesh and blood of the animals they eat; for the last thought of the animal was of pain and violence and death, which taints their very flesh; and for those who eat such as this, there can never be peace of long duration, for the very food they eat causes an unrighteous temper to simmer in their heart and mind and come quickly to anger and violence.

7 But I will share with you now a great secret: If you desire peace that never ends, then among those who desire such, I say unto you, kill no creatures whatsoever. Eat only of the plants God has put onto the earth to sustain you and foods made from the milk and eggs of the animals loved as friends and not caged and of the honey of the bees. Then a spirit of peace shall prevail over you always."

8 And one of the warriors was exceedingly wroth with Yeshua and said, "I do not desire a peaceful spirit, for of what good would that be when my town is attacked? And how can you dare say it is wrong for me to kill the

beasts that I might feed my family?"

9 Yeshua answered him calmly, saying, "Even the gentle will find a fire in their heart to defend their family. And when there is no enemy at the gate, a peaceful heart makes for a fruitful community.

10 And I say unto you that God has put all the animals of the earth and all the fishes of the sea and all the birds of the air and everything that lives upon the earth to be used by man with thanksgiving, as man has vital need of them. And nothing is forbidden to you by God for food or clothing or shelter, even unto all creatures upon the earth, if there is nothing else to give unto your family.

11 But God has also made man a steward and a protector of all the lesser creatures of the earth and is pleased if their lives are never taken save there is no other way to preserve your own.

12 Verily, each time you take the life of a higher creature, those that nurture their young, you are not only killing them and taking them from their family, but you are also killing yourself and taking yourself from your family before your time.

13 But each time you eat a meal of the fresh plants and nuts and seeds and the herbs that God has put upon the earth to be food for man, you add days to your life.

14 Instead of killing the animals and eating their flesh, look to them to be your friends and under your protection and concern, to be used to help you with your labors, to give you fibers for your clothing and food from their milk and new eggs.

15 Look at the feast before you; see the great amounts of fresh food from your fields and your waters and your

trees and the foods that you have made from the milk and eggs of the animals. This God has given you in great abundance, and it is life unto you and meat unto you, and it is ever renewed by God; therefore, what need is there to kill the higher creatures of the earth, who bond to their family as you do to yours and who simply seek peace in their lives even as you do?"

16 And Yeshua's words strongly affected some of the people insomuch that they put down the meat that was at their lips and looked to one another with the light of a new understanding in their mind and heart. But others were still wroth, and some berated him, saying, "How can these animals be his friends? For we killed them a day to the south, and he knew them not."

17 And thus it was that some did marvel because of Yeshua and others did grumble.

SECOND SERMON IN BETHANY

Excerpted from the Oracles of Celestine Light: Vivus: Chapter 1

And it came to pass that Yeshua and Miriam returned to the land of Palestine and journeyed to Bethany so that they might see again their friends and family that dwelt there.

2 Miriam's family was overcome with joy when she arrived and embraced her and the children with tears of happiness. Her father called for a feast to be held, and from the first moment of their arrival, there was much merriment and celebration.

3 Many people from the town soon came to the house of Miriam's father when they heard that Yeshua of Nazareth had returned. Among some, he was held to be a prophet and among others, a master storyteller. Still others felt he was a rabbi of great knowledge, while more than a few considered him sacrilegious and a blasphemer. But among all, even those who disdained him, there was an anticipation to be able to hear his engaging and intriguing words again.

4 Yochanan and Martha soon joined them, as did Lazarus and Hannah, and the children of several families played together while their parents renewed everlasting bonds of friendship, love, and faith forged in unforgettable mutual experiences.

5. For three days, the welcoming feast continued and crowds gathered each day, hoping to hear Yeshua speak. But each day Lazarus came to them and told them that Yeshua would not speak that day.

6 After seeing the disappointment in the faces of so many people he knew, Lazarus went to Yeshua and beseeched him to say something to the townspeople else they begin to have their good joy of anticipation turn into the anger of frustration.

7 Yeshua explained his reluctance, saying, "Lazarus, my good brother of spirit, I do not wish to make a host of enemies before my time, for it will come soon enough. Though my teachings will bring the elect to God, they will only inflame the pious and anger the unrighteous. That is well and as it should be, but before the persecutions begin, there are still many things I must do and wish to do, in quiet and peace."

8 Upon hearing the words of Yeshua, Lazarus pleaded all the more, saying, "But these are my friends and the friends of my family, and they are here at our feast, at your feast. It would honor us if you would impart your wisdom among us. I know they will not vilify you even if they disagree with your words. And perhaps there is one among them whose life will be changed, who will find the Celestine Light of Elohim, this day, because of the things you say."

9 Yeshua was greatly moved by the words of Lazarus, and he told him, "God has truly touched your heart, Lazarus, for you have spoken words of might and right. Let us go even now to the courtyard to see if the winnow of my words will uncover the pure grain from the chaff."

10 And it came to pass that Yeshua entered the
courtyard of the house of the Father of Lazarus and
stood upon the large fountain at the center as a crowd of
friends and family and townspeople gathered beneath
him.
11 And he said unto them, "Good people of Bethany, I
and my family are honored to be among you once more.
I am humbled by your desire to hear my words and may
each of you find the lamp you need to light the darkness
before you.
12 While my family and I traveled in Egypt, we came
to know wonderful people of many different nations
and races and religions. Despite the differences in their
character, they had many good things in common.
13 Whatever the color of their skin, they loved their
children. Whether they were Egyptian or Roman
or Hebrew, they desired to please the God of their
understanding. Whether they were rich or poor, they
sought good things for their family. Whether they
were city dwellers or desert nomads, they showed us
friendship and hospitality.
14 Only among the zealots of every religion did we
find harsh judgment and even hatred spit out upon
everyone who believed not as they did, sometimes so
much so that to take a man's life in the name of their
God seemed to them very reasonable.
15 Yet these same men also loved their children and
desired good things for their family. When among those
who believed as they did, they were honorable and of
good character.
16 How then can it be that the precepts of religion

or loyalty to tribe or country can cause a man to act in ways that are repugnant to his very soul?

17 Is man's soul at war with itself? Even in your own home, do you find that sometimes you are a dutiful and considerate father and husband or a caring and loving mother and wife, but then at another moment, you say or do things to those whom you love which cause them pain and grief and your own soul, anguish because of that which you have done? Is your soul at war with itself?

18 When you see the clouds begin to gather upon the mountain slope, you know that rains will soon come. But it is not because of the clouds that the rain will fall, but because of the mountain.

19 If the mountain were instead a plain, the clouds would pass on by. But they are blocked in their progress by the wall of the mountain, and the clouds continue to gather and thicken upon the slopes until a storm is brewed.

20 So it is with you. Your immortal soul is a piece of the Celestine Light of Elohim. It is the cloud in its whiteness and purity. For the breath of eternity that you dwell upon this earth, your mortal body is the mountain. And the pure cloud of your soul cannot avoid the impure mountain of your mortal life any more than the clouds of the sky can avoid confronting the mountains of the earth.

21 The war is not within your soul any more than the cloud is at war with itself. It is the encounter with the mountain that causes the storm, even as your own soul is ever at odds with the natural man that is the rawness

of the physical.

22 All things have been made by God. Therefore, I declare to you that it is Elohim that has made man to be at war with himself, to be tempted by evil even as he is prompted by the light of God within his own soul to forsake evil and do only good.

23 Verily, this quandary God has given to man that man might overcome himself and discover and follow the Celestine Light of Elohim within his soul.

24 In this, man becomes more than he was, and for this cause has Elohim created all the heavens and the earth and put man upon it, that he might become more than he began.

25 Who then is the adversary? Where is the root of evil that continually torments and tempts man? It is you. Man is his own enemy.

26 To conquer yourself in a far greater measure than you are conquered by yourself is the supreme challenge of life, and only those who succeed will pass the portal of harmonic judgment into eternal glory.

27 Verily, the first door to the first Heaven is only opened by a worthy life. Riches cannot open it, except the richness given in a life of service to others.

28 Living the law and only the law cannot open it, except the law to love God with all of your heart, and if it is so, then your love is shown in the good you do for your mother and your father, your wives and your children, and your fellow men upon the earth.

29 Each day, you must choose who will be your master, the light of your soul or the darkness of your earthly body. Each hour, you must choose to listen to the quiet

voice within you, the Celestine Light of Elohim, or give into the temptations of the dark weakness within your body. But remember, nothing is hidden from God.

30 Therefore, choose wisely, for you know not the day or the hour that your life ends and your eternity begins. Whether you rise to eternal glory or fall into the long darkness of desolation depends upon the lamp of brightness or the cold chains of misery you forged for yourself in life, for thus you pass by your resonance through the harmonic portal of judgment into your eternity.

31 Elohim gave you the instrument of your body, but you are the musician that decides the music your life will play.

32 And I say unto you that when you see a man showing goodness and light by his actions, you can know regardless of his color or his tribe or his religion or even his conception of God that he is heeding the promptings of the Celestine Light of Elohim, which resides in his soul, that he is growing closer to Heaven, and that God is well pleased with this man at this moment.

33 Likewise, when you see a man that is acting in darkness, disobeying the commandments of Elohim and disrespecting himself, or his family, or his fellow men, regardless of who he is or what he believes, then you can know with a certainty that this man, at this moment, has forsaken the Celestine Light of Elohim that resides eternally in his soul and has heeded the empty promptings of the lower mortal man that feeds his desires but gives him no succor.

34 Verily, this dance of light and darkness is of greater importance to your eternity than you know, and you dance it every day of your life."

35 Then Obadiah of Bethany rose to speak and said unto Yeshua, "I am a good and pious man. I am faithful to my family and to my God. I am not perfect, but I think all among us will acknowledge that I am a good and godly man. You would make it seem as if I am always at war with myself, and such is not the case."

36 Yeshua smiled warmly and answered, "Your heart is surely good, Obadiah, and your actions speak louder than words that you strive each day to live your life in ways that are pleasing to God. But did you come out of the womb such a good man?"

37 "No, I did not," Obadiah answered, "I have been taught from an early age in the ways I should go and I have strived mightily to follow the good things I have been taught. In my youth I sometimes made foolish choices, but I have learned from my errors, even those I repeated because I did not fully understand them at first."

38 Yeshua smiled and said unto him, "Verily, you are fulfilling the desires of Elohim. It is for this cause, that you might perfect yourself, that God has given unto you and all men and women this life in mortality.

39 That you are a better person in your old age than you were in your youth bears witness that the Celestine Light of your soul has shown through the darkness of your mortality.

40 Yet even today in the wisdom of your years and the fortitude of your experiences, are you not still tempted

to sometimes raise your voice in unrighteous anger, to sometimes not say all that you know if it could be to your advantage, even while it is to another man's disadvantage?"

41 Obadiah wrung his hands as he silently sought to control his displeasure at the words Yeshua had spoken, and he said, "While it may be true that I sometimes think to speak in anger, as I did even now, and sometimes think of an advantage I would gain by my silence that would be lost by my speaking, in my old age, I no longer give into such temptations; I speak only with respect and calm, even if I am in turmoil in my heart. And I speak the truth to my fellow men, even when my silence would not be dishonest."

42 Yeshua smiled again and there was on his face a great contentment, and he said unto Obadiah, "Verily, you are dancing even now, as I have spoken. Thus do all men and women. This is the never-ending dance of perfection. It is the dance of light and darkness. It is your lower mortal man tempting you to darkness, but your higher man heeding your eternal soul calling you to the light that is your birthright.

43 Each day, your lower man invites you to eat what you should not eat, to say what you should not say, and to do what you should not do, all things which lead to an empty cup, no matter how many times you fill it.

44 And every moment, step by step, your higher man, which is the Celestine Light of Elohim in your soul, whispers in your ear, touches your heart, and asks you to turn from darkness and choose the light, to eat what you should eat, to say what you should say, and to do

what you should do.

45 The day will come when you will stand before Elohim and be judged by the resonance you have danced in life, with all things revealed, both your virtues and your weaknesses and your sins. And you shall inherit the resonance in eternity that you chose, both openly and in secret, in life.

46 Therefore, let each man and each woman remember that every step you take, every word you speak, and every deed you do is inscribed in either the Book of Light or the Book of Darkness.

47 On the Judgment Day, Elohim will take the pages from the books, and they shall be weighed in the balance to see if you are found wanting."

48 Then rose Saul the Shepherd from among the crowd, and he asked, "What of one such as me? I am ashamed to say I have lived a very ungodly life for most of my years as many amongst us know. I am sorry for so many of the things I have said and done, but I cannot take them back. Now I am an old man, and by your words am I to understand that I am condemned in Heaven while I still yet live in mortality? Is there nothing I can do?"

49 Yeshua was touched by his humbleness of heart, and he said unto him, "Elohim takes deep joy in the repentant sinner, and from a true repentance, you are born again; the record of the Book of Darkness is taken away, never to be seen again for the years that came before, for your resonance has changed, as long as your repentance is true, and you continue to walk in the light, with faith in the love and justice of Elohim, from

that day forth.

50 What then is a true repentance that is so great that Elohim would remove the record of your sins in the Book of Darkness? Verily, it is this: that you would feel a sorrow that grieves your heart and brings tears of shame to your eyes, that you would pray to Elohim and confess all of your sins acknowledging your error, promising to sin no more, and humbly asking for forgiveness.

51 Then you must prove the truth of your repentance by seeking out the people you have sinned against, be it small or great, and confess your sins to them or to their posterity if they have passed on and, as much as is possible, make restitution for the darkness you have done.

52 Yet for some things, because of the sin or the circumstances, there can be no direct restitution. For these, you must make amends in the best way that the light of Elohim whispers to your heart is right and just.

53 Repentance is not easy, nor is it done in a day; but it is given to all men and women that once they find again the Celestine Light within their heart, mind, and soul, they may put it in a lamp that will burn from everlasting to everlasting.

54 But I say unto you, do not procrastinate the day of your repentance, for the days of your mortality are numbered, and very small they are. You know not upon which day Elohim will call for your soul and open the Books of Light and Darkness to weigh your life in the balance to discover the resonance of your soul."

55 Hearing this, Saul the Shepherd fell on his knees upon the ground and, crying out with a loud voice,

asked God to forgive him for his sins and promised to live in the light of Elohim from that day forth.

56 Then he arose and immediately went among the crowd and began to confess to them sins he had done to them in the past, to express his deep sorrow for his wrong, and to ask their forgiveness. And many were the embraces of love and friendship that came forth from those to whom he spoke.

57 But some among the people were affronted by the words of Yeshua and thought to themselves that they needed no repentance, for they were descendants of Abraham and Isaac and obeyed all the letters of the laws.

58 And from among them arose Yagur the Pharisee and he said unto Yeshua, "By what authority do you say these things? Which prophets are you quoting that we may know that your words are of true merit?

59 In truth, we know all the prophets and you do not speak their words, but seem to be creating your own. We know the prophets, but we know not you. So by what authority do you speak things that have never before been spoken?"

60 And Yeshua looked down upon Yagur and said unto him, "I speak by the authority of Elohim, and it is from the words of Elohim that I speak. Hear my words, O men of the world, for by them you will be justified, and by them you will be condemned."

61 And many were stunned by the words of Yeshua, for he spoke with power and authority such as they had never before heard.

62 And they turned to whisper to one another, saying, "Surely, this man must be a great prophet, for he speaks

with the calmness of still waters, the confidence of a lion, and the power of thunder. He does not quote the prophets that came before, but speaks as if he has been given the words from the very mouth of Elohim."

63 Yagur paled because of the words of Yeshua, but still rose to contend with him again, saying, "The time of the great prophets has passed, and you are blasphemous to speak as you do. You do not speak to uphold the laws that have been given, as a true prophet would, but think to make new laws unto yourself.

64 And more, you speak in ways that are contrary to the law, for you have spoken that even those who are not a part of us, not one of the chosen, can still find equal favor with Elohim, simply because they live a good life.

65 You have spoken of the commandments of Sinai, but then speak as if the law is nothing more than living a life of service. To me, it seems as if you say one thing, then contradict it with the very next breath. And in almost all things you have said, you speak at odds with that which is sacred and holy and has been so from Abraham to our fathers."

66 Yeshua answered him firmly, "Every child born of woman is the chosen of Elohim, for they are all the children of God, and Elohim does not favor one over the other from their birth, any more than you should favor one of your children over another from the time they are born.

67 It has been the custom to favor the firstborn and to give unto them the greatest opportunities and inheritance. Although this may conserve the family's wealth, where is the fairness to the siblings of the first?

Are they less deserving simply because they came out of their mother's womb upon a later day?

68 And if the first son should grow into a man of darkness while his brothers and sisters grow into men and women of light, where is the fairness to give all that a family has as an inheritance to the first?

69 Which is more important, preserving the family's wealth even if it is given unto darkness or using the wealth to uplift the righteous and reward those that walk in light?

70 Verily, I say unto you: Elohim does not reward the wicked simply because of their lineage, and those who say it is so speak as men cloaking their falsehoods in piety to justify themselves

71 Be they king or pauper, the only reward for the wicked in the Kingdom of Heaven is desolation.

72 When a child grows into an age of understanding and accountability, their sins are not overlooked by virtue of their lineage, but only by virtue of contrite repentance.

73 Neither are they rewarded because of their lineage, but only because of sincere acts of devotion and kindness, worthy of praise and great blessings.

74 So it is with the blessings of Elohim upon all men. Each reaps what they sow, not what their fathers sowed, not what the prophets of their faith sowed, but only what they sowed, each and every day of their life.

75 And what think you of the commandments of Sinai? Were they given to be a prison for man or a freedom? I say unto you that Elohim asks nothing of man except to live in ways that would help man to grow

into the Celestine Light that Elohim gave to him.

76 So it is with the commandments of Sinai. A man may live them all and follow every letter of the law, but if he does so grudgingly, then in his heart, he obeys none of them, and on the Day of Judgment, he will be weighed in the balance by the sincerity of his heart, not the pretense of his actions.

77 But any man who loves God with the depth of his heart also loves all that lives because Elohim has made it, and this man will live the commandments of Sinai, even if he is from a far land and has never heard of them.

78 Because he loves God, including the light of God that is within him, and respects and cherishes all the life that Elohim has put upon the earth, to live the commandments, even unseen and unknown, is as natural for this man as every breath he takes.

79 And Elohim loves him and favors him, not because of who his father was, nor whether he was the firstborn or the last, nor whether he is a Hebrew or a Gentile, but because of who he has chosen to become inside himself, because of how he has chosen to live both seen and unseen by men, because of the light he gives unto the world.

80 Verily, I say unto you that all who are humble, repent of their sins, and always strive to live in the light shall be blessed with peace in their heart and true friends beyond price.

81 Their faithfulness and goodness in life will open the doors to the glory of Heaven, and in eternity, they shall reap the everlasting harvest of the good seeds they have sown.

82 Before you sleep this night, look upon yourself. Among men, only you know your true heart. But Elohim knows all. Therefore, that which you cannot hide from God, hide no longer from yourself, nor support that which is wrong by contriving to justify how it is right.

83 Vow unto yourself a sacred promise to raise the lamp of the Celestine Light of Elohim that resides in your soul and henceforth always walk with your light held high that darkness can no more dwell within you.

84 You are the master. The light of your soul contends with the temptations of your body. Choose to be the master of your body instead of its slave, and you will find a joy and peace in this world such as you never have imagined and a great reward in Heaven, beyond the descriptions of men, built with every good you have ever sown."

85 Then Yeshua came down from the fountain and walked among them. And many were the men and women who touched him and asked blessings upon him, and many were those whom he touched and blessed with a portion of his light.

TEACHINGS IN CAPHARSALAMA

Excerpted from the Oracles of Celestine Light: Vivus: Chapter 4

And it came to pass that the family of Yochanan remained in Bethany at the house of Martha's parents, under the stewardship of her brother Lazarus, while Yochanan bid them farewell and made a journey to Gimron.

2 And Yeshua and Miriam began a journey with their two children to Nazareth so that they might once again see the family of Yeshua.

3 Their farewells to their family and friends in Bethany were prolonged, causing them to depart late in the morning. A donkey carried their belongings, and they traveled slowly by foot because of the children. After a short first day's journey, they set a camp for the evening, some distance from the road, on the north side of the village of Capharsalama.

4 As Miriam was preparing the evening meal of bread from Bethany and salad from greens they had picked along their route, they saw a man running along the road, being pursued by three other men who caught up with him as they watched and began to beat him with short sticks.

5 "Stay here with the children," Yeshua commanded. Then without another word, he ran toward the

altercation.

6 As he came upon the men, they did not even notice him, so intent were they upon beating the hapless fellow on the ground, who was looking up at the stars and calling out in a weak voice, "God is great. Help me, O Lord."

7 Coming beside them unnoticed, Yeshua said in a loud voice of exceeding power, "In the name of Elohim, cease this instant your cowardly deed!"

8 Hearing a voice of thunder coming as seemed to them from the very air around them caused all three of the attackers such fright that they let go of their sticks as if they were hot irons and dropped to the ground trembling in fear.

9 Ignoring them, Yeshua went to assist the man they had been beating. Blood flowed freely from his head and his body, and he moaned softly with his eyes closed. Yeshua knelt beside him and touched his wounded head lightly. Immediately, the bleeding stopped.

10 Yeshua looked up at his attackers, saying, "As his clothes show, this man is poor, so you do not beat him to steal his money. But you have nearly taken his life. For what cause think you to take the authority of God into your hands?"

11 The three men rose up, and seeing Yeshua alone and weaponless, their courage began to return. The largest pointed a finger at the stricken man and said, "He is not from our village, and we have seen that he has unnatural affections for men, which thing we cannot abide.

12 It was only last week that our rabbi exhorted us

that it is an abomination for a man to lie with another and such should be put to death. We are devout men, not just in word, but also in deed, and we are here to fulfill the will of God."

13 Yeshua stood up, and in his height, he was taller than the largest of the attackers, and he said unto them, "Has this man sinned against you?" And the three denied that he had. And Yeshua said, "Has he sinned against your family?" And again, they denied that he had. And Yeshua asked once more, "Then how is it that you say he has sinned?"

14 The middle of the three became flustered and, speaking quickly, said, "He was found sleeping in a stable under a cloak with another man. The other ran faster than we could catch, but this one we have. Therefore, leave us be and we will finish what we have begun."

15 "They were naked beneath the cloak?" Yeshua inquired. And the men replied that they had been clothed. "Then how was it that they were showing affection one for another?" Yeshua wondered. But again, the men said they did not see such.

16 "Perhaps, they were merely drawing closer to share warmth on a cold night." Yeshua suggested. "And they are not after all as you assume them to be.

17 As you judge so shall you be judged by Elohim.

18 If you take a life, especially from a false judgment, it is you who will stand condemned before God and pay for your sins, not just with your life, but with your eternity. Are you so sure of your judgment then that you will risk your own eternal reward?"

19 The men looked upon the ground and shuffled about sheepishly, mumbling to one another at the words Yeshua had said and unsure how to answer.

20 Yeshua admonished them, "Return now to your homes and leave this man, for you know neither the will nor the power of Elohim. I will return to Capharsalama in the morning and will speak to your rabbi. Let him know that Yeshua of Nazareth will call upon him after the morning meal."

21 Then the men backed away from Yeshua and, turning about, hurried back to their village to speak of all that had transpired.

22 Yeshua squatted down, and putting his arms beneath the limp body of the man, he easily lifted him and carried him to where Miriam and the children waited.

23 Miriam tended to the man's wounds with water and herbs while Yeshua explained that even though their first day had been a short journey, their second day would be even shorter, as they must return to Capharsalama in the morning so that he might speak to the rabbi.

24 They had no campfire, but there was a bright Moon that night. After the children fell into sleep, Miriam applied fresh crushed herbs to the man's wounds, and Yeshua came to him and touched him lightly at each spot of his injuries, saying, "As you love God, may your wounds so be healed."

25 The man slept soundly through the night and awakened upon the sunrise, startled to see he was still alive, lying with a family about him and his attackers

nowhere to be seen. "What miracle has occurred that I am here?" he asked in amazement.

26 Yeshua came to him and, putting his hand upon his shoulder, said, "I am Yeshua of Nazareth and this is my wife Miriam, and our children, Uriel and Dara. Yesterday was not your day to die, and your greatness is still before you."

27 Then Yeshua told him of all that had befallen him from the moment he was hit on the head and fell asleep until the moment he had just now awakened.

28 After listening to Yeshua, the man shook his head dejectedly saying, "I am Ephres, and I have no greatness before me. I have nothing. I am nothing, except miserable. In truth, I am guilty of what my attackers accused me of, so leave me; I am grateful for your help, but now you know the truth, so do not waste your time with one such as me."

29 Despite his words, Yeshua did not move, and he told him, "I have always known the truth. And Elohim is more concerned with the virtues of your character and the faithfulness of your devotion than the choices of your affections. Though you may be scorned by the ignorant, you are loved by God."

30 The words of Yeshua were like the greatest balm of healing to Ephres. A smile of wonder came upon his face, and he glowed with serenity from within his heart. He looked upon Yeshua with awe and told him, "If only all men felt as you do, I could lead a normal life."

31 "There is no other way a man who loves and gives true devotion to Elohim could feel," Yeshua answered. "I am going now to speak with the rabbi and the people

of Capharsalama that they may have no confusion on this. If you are well enough, I would like you to come with me and my family."

32 "Of course!" Ephres said in eagerness, standing up quickly, to his own surprise. "You are my savior, and even now go to defend me. I would be less than an ant if I did not stand beside you."

33 After Ephres had eaten a little bread with honey and olive oil, he stood thumping his chest and exclaimed, "I feel like a new man. In truth, I do not even have bruises upon my body. How can this be?"

34 And Yeshua said unto him, "In your darkest hour, you did not call upon men for mercy, but upon God for strength. Even as you have asked, so it has been done, because of your faith."

35 Shortly thereafter, Yeshua, Miriam, their children, and Ephres returned to Capharsalama.

36 As they walked toward the village, they did not have to seek out the rabbi, for their approach had been noted by the villagers and the rabbi and several of the men from the village stood upon the road awaiting them.

37 As they approached, the rabbi raised his hand, saying, "Stop there. You may not enter this village if you walk with this wretch of a man or with a brazen woman who is not covered, for God has said that it is an abomination for a man to lie with another and a shame for a women to be uncovered among men."

38 Despite the bravado of the rabbi and the courage instilled by their numbers, the gathered men still seemed somewhat in awe of Yeshua, for his presence, even

without speaking, was powerful and unusual. Because of his height, all upon the road looked up to him, and his hair, though not long, was longer than usually seen among the men of Judea.

39 Because of the influence of the Greeks and Romans, many men his age removed their facial hair, but he wore a full beard, which was a little longer than the current fashion and slightly parted in the middle in a style seldom seen. Lastly, his eyes were a most piercing blue, a rare color in Palestine and unnerving to many who looked upon him.

40 Facing the men, Yeshua held out his arms to his sides, at waist height with his palms forward, saying, "Rabbi, by what law do you bar our passage, condemn this man, and vilify my wife?"

41 And the Rabbi answered, "By the Code of Moses."

42 Taking a moment to look individually at each man in the group, which had a diverse appearance, Yeshua further inquired, "The same code that says that men should not cut their hair or beard?"

43 The rabbi seemed irritated by the question, answering, "There is only one Code of Moses, but there are degrees of graveness; whether one's hair is short or long, whether one has a beard or not, is not comparable with sexual transgressions, particularly the most heinous kind that this man is guilty of."

44 Now Yeshua spoke calmly and quietly, but with great power in his voice, saying, "And I declare unto you that the Code of Moses is only in small part from Moses and more from men who knew not God.

45 And by this, you may know the truth: If a law

teaches to honor and respect Elohim and to honor and respect yourself and to honor and respect your fellow brothers and sisters of spirit upon this earth, and to honor and respect all creatures over which you are stewards, then you may know with a certainty that it is from God.

46 But if it teaches to not honor and respect Elohim, or to not honor and respect yourself, or to not honor and respect your fellow brothers and sisters of spirit, or to not honor and respect life entrusted to your stewardship, then you may know with certainty that it is of man, and any who obey it do so to appease man, not God."

47 The crowd stood unable to move, shocked that any man could say such things. And the rabbi, after his gaping mouth closed, began to sputter in a most angry manner, saying, "This is blasphemy of the highest order. How dare you speak such horrible words? God shall surely strike you where you stand."

48 With a smile, Yeshua looked about him to the sky, as if waiting for a thunderbolt to come from Heaven. And he told them, "If I were speaking that which was not true, then surely I could not stand before you and would suffer the wrath of Heaven. But here I still stand, and I say unto you that the spirit of God is in me, and I speak the truth to you. Therefore, open your ears that you may hear."

49 Now the rabbi was still sorely vexed at the words of Yeshua and was about to respond with a condemnation when Yeshua interjected, saying, "Prove me now, good men of Capharsalama. If I can show you that the Code of

Moses is more a code of men than of God, will you then consider that the words which are written concerning women and men may not be after all the truth as you have always been taught?"

50 Hearing this statement from Yeshua, the rabbi practically screamed, "Sacrilege! The Code of Moses was given by the word of God. To say it is not perfect in every way is to say God is not perfect."

51 Yeshua answered, "If all the words which are written came from Elohim through Moses, then you would be correct as would your judgments upon us. But are you so afraid of truth that you will not even allow me to prove to you that the words you hold sacred are often the greatest sacrilege?"

52 "We will not listen to such nonsense," the rabbi proclaimed.

53 But one of the men of the village stepped forward and said, "Let us hear the words of the stranger, for he speaks as one who has authority. If we judge his words to be in error, then we are no worse off and he will be exposed as an affront to God. But if we judge his words to be wise, then we will have gained something of importance on this day."

54 The rabbi glared at the man and began to speak in anger again, but seeing the crowd in agreement with the words of the villager, he acquiesced to Yeshua, "Very well, speak as you will, but know that your very words will be your condemnation."

55 Yeshua looked one by one into the eyes of each man before him and then said unto them, "If the Code of Moses were actually written by Moses as given unto him

by Elohim, then it could contain no errors of substance.

56 If it were written only by Moses and no others, there could be no confusion. If it were written by a prophet of God, it would only contain that which leads men to honor and respect God and the creations, which God has made.

57 To prove that some of the laws are of man, I will first show that many of the words written in the books of Moses are from unnamed men other than Moses, for if they fall, so fall the erroneous laws which they contain.

58 Good Rabbi, can you tell me, was Moses a humble man?"

59 And the Rabbi frowned, answering, "The word of God says, the man Moses was very meek, above all the men who were upon the face of the earth."

60 Yeshua inquired further of him, "And in his humility, he wrote these words about himself?"

61 Perhaps, a later writer added that little tribute," the rabbi admitted.

62 And what think you men of Capharsalama?" Yeshua continued. "The Torah also says there arose not a prophet since like unto Moses, whom the Lord knew face-to-face. Did Moses in his humility, write his own eulogy?"

63 And the men of Capharsalama murmured that these were indeed questions.

64 But the rabbi said, "These are trivial things. You speak of nothing of substance."

65 "Then perhaps you will consider the covenant with Abraham significant, as there are different accounts of this blessing from which all the Children of Israel claim

their birthright.

66 Or perhaps the name of God, which Moses surely knew, but which is said differently in different parts of the Torah, as is the important account of the revelation at Beth-el to Jacob from which the Children of Israel claim the land of their forefathers.

67 And what of the commandments of Sinai? Are they so complex that Moses must write them twice and differently each time?

68 And what of women? Are they chattel or servants or merely comely beasts to be used as man sees fit? The books of Moses give a record of Lot, a man so righteous that God spared him, but destroyed all the inhabitants of Sodom and Gomorrah.

69 Yet according to the sacred books, just shortly before, Lot offered his two virgin daughters to be raped by an unsavory group of townspeople rather than let them speak to the men who were visiting his house.

70 And what of the recordings of genocide, those places where the books of Moses record God commanding that every man, woman, and child of an enemy should be killed?

71 O men of Capharsalama, consider the feelings in your heart, even as your mind considers my words. Would you give your daughters up to strangers to be raped? Do you think Elohim, the true God of Heaven and earth, would ask you to do such a thing?

72 And if you were in an army that came upon a village of innocent women and children, even babes upon their mother's breast, could you strike them down as they fled or pleaded for mercy and kill them? Do you

think that Elohim, the true God of Heaven and earth, would ever ask you to do such a thing?

73 Think not that I speak only of the errors of the books of Moses, for many are the errors of men in the books that came after Moses.

74 Is it not written in the law that you shall not suffer a witch to live? Yet is it not also written that King Saul sought council of the witch of Endor and that she made manifest the dead prophet Samuel, that the king might speak with him when neither God nor the prophets in his Kingdom would? Or has that part been kept from you in the readings of the sacred books?

75 Know you not that if this were so, it would make a witch greater than a prophet of God? Verily, it would make a witch greater than God, for God would not come to Saul in dreams and the prophets of God spoke to him not. Yet it is written that by the power of the witch, Samuel was made manifest, and by the power of the witch, the prophet of God spoke.

76 O men of Capharsalama, these are not the words or actions of Elohim. They are the abominations of men seduced by familiar spirits to write that which is contrary to the very nature of God.

77 Therefore, O men of Capharsalama, consider the words that I have spoken of all these things that are contained within the books of Moses.

78 I say unto you that these writings are the evil desires and commandments of men.

79 They are not possible for a God of infinite love and fairness, and they are not worthy of you."

80 "It is you who speaks sly abominations upon that

which is sacred" the rabbi said. "These are weighty matters which confuse those not well versed in the law and cannot be properly addressed by a handful of common men on a village road during the heat of the midday. These are fine points fit only for those trained in the law to comprehend. In any case, the main messages of the law and the sacred books are indisputable, even if there were discrepancies, which I do not say is true."

81 And Yeshua said unto him, "The true words of Elohim are simple and clear to all men and need not the interpretation of priests, for God would ask nothing of man that could not be easily understood by all, lest man error because of misunderstanding and not through willful disobedience.

82 The true laws of Elohim are meant to be a freedom to man, to establish simple, clear paths of righteousness by which man may prosper when he walks the path.

83 The unrighteous laws of men, both those given by Caesar and those given by priests, are intended to be an enslavement to man, to compel him to give of his time and substance to sustain those in power, to put fear of punishments into his heart, that he can be controlled and will obey dictates of the unrighteous laws which his spirit would otherwise give no concern to or value.

84 Therefore, what man has perverted, let me make clear, and in this listen to the spirit of God that resides within each of you, within every man and woman ever born, for this quiet voice will always testify to you of truth if you will open your heart and mind to receive it."

85 "Of this man," he said pointing to Ephres, "think you that it matters to Elohim to whom he directs

the affections of his heart as long as he gives his first devotion to God?

86 And if he gives his first devotion to God, it must follow as night to day that he also does good to all men, for a man devoted to Elohim has only peace and love in his heart.

87 To give sincere devotion to God and to give good in your words and actions to your brothers and sisters of spirit is all that God asks of anyone. Any law that demands other than this speaks not from God, but from man.

88 And think you that it is a shame that my wife is uncovered? Would you also cover the glory of the sun or the Moon or the stars? For they too are God's creations.

89 Woman was made to stand beside man, not behind him; equal to him, not less than him; thus have they been made by Elohim."

90 At this, the rabbi could not contain himself and said, "Numerous are the places in the Law where a woman's place is given. She is clearly under the direction of her husband.

91 And no man of worth wants to see another man lusting after his wife, so it must be that she is well covered when in public. This is just common sense if nothing else."

92 Yeshua took a step toward the rabbi, saying, "Verily, I say unto you any man who would make a woman less than a man, or subject to the will of a man, will find desolation in the world to come.

93 Elohim has made them equal in this life and the life to come. Look you to the books of Moses, which

you love, and the story of creation: When Adam and Eve were given the Garden of Eden, God did not give dominion of all the earth only to man, but to both man and woman equally.

94 And thus it is so: Man and woman are equal in the sight of God and whosoever would have dominion over woman in this life acts from an evil heart, and not the true light of God."

95 The mouth of the rabbi gaped again as he prepared to speak, but before he could speak his mind, Yeshua said unto all of the men, "I have said what I have said. I have given you the true Celestine Light of God. How then will you now act? What does your heart feel? What is the truth that whispers in your mind despite all you have been taught before?

96 Here we will leave you, for my family journeys north. But I say unto you that this man, Ephres, is a good and righteous man who is devoted to God and does only good to his fellow man. Will you let him pass your town in peace?"

97 The rabbi blustered, "Nothing you have said has changed anything. Good riddance to you and take that man with you if you do not desire him to meet a worse fate."

98 But the villager who had spoken before stepped forth again, saying, "The rabbi does not speak for all of us. My heart and I think the hearts of some of my friends have been touched by the words you have said. You have given us much to consider.

99 We are not changed from who we were to who you would have us be in these short moments, but we have

changed enough to give more thought to the words you have spoken.

100 Therefore, go your way in peace and forgive us the disrespect to your wife. The man Ephres may come in peace to our village. None will harm him."

101 At those words, the rabbi turned in disgust and walked back toward the village.

102 And Yeshua came forward and put his hand upon the shoulder of the villager who had spoken, asking, "What is your name, friend?"

103 "I am called Gimiel," he replied. "I am a simple man with flocks of sheep."

104 Yeshua smiled, saying, "Your humility has not hidden your courage, nor your simpleness the sharpness of your mind. I return to my home in Galilee, and the time will soon come when you shall hear of me again. If you know then what you know not now, come to me, and you shall learn the mysteries of the Kingdom of God."

105 Gimiel bowed his head to Yeshua and said unto him, "Teacher, you have opened our eyes today, but now you depart and we will have no one to give us further knowledge. Lest we soon fall back into our old ways, how then are we to know that which is true from that which is false when we are confronted with a choice?"

106 Yeshua answered, saying, "When you see a fine carpet from the masters of Tarsus, you have no doubt of its authenticity because of the tightness of the weave, the brightness of the colors, the purity of the wool, the subtle highlights of the silk, and the beauty of the design.

107 If a man were to come to you and offer to sell you

a carpet he said was from Tarsus, it would take you but a moment of examination to know whether the carpet merchant spoke truth.

108 So it is with the words of God as spoken by prophets and prophetesses through all time and the corruption of the words of men upon the sacred.

109 Like the carpets of Tarsus, the true words of God are built upon a foundation that marks them undeniably as to their source.

110 In this, you have a most easy test. You do not have to get into great theological contemplations, for the ways of God are pure and simple, distinct and easy to know.

111 The commandments of Sinai have been given to you, and they are easy to live. The very first words of God as recorded spoken to Adam and Eve are in innocent purity, as yet undiluted by the machinations of men.

112 Therefore, if the commandments say not to kill, but in other places in the sacred books it records the people of God being commanded to kill every man, woman, and child, is this not a contradiction of the foundation of truth?

113 If Elohim told Adam and Eve that every herb bearing seed, which is upon the face of all the earth, and every tree in which is the fruit of a tree yielding seed would be meat for them, but later the sacred books record God saying to eat the flesh of animals, is this not a contradiction of the foundation of truth, in both the commandments of Sinai and the word of Elohim spoken to Adam and Eve?

114 Do you think that Elohim is a changeable God who gives contradicting commandments or conforms to the desires of men? Verily, I say no! Elohim is the same yesterday, today, and forever.

115 Seek to understand the heart and essence of Elohim, and you will hold the foundation of good by which you may know the truth of all things of light.

116 Here then is the key to understand the foundation of Elohim, whereby you may know the truth of all things of God: Verily, the basis of all goodness and godliness is to love and respect God, the giver of all life and the creator of all things.

117 And to love and respect your neighbors, for every injury to them is an injury to you and every blessing to them is a blessing to you.

118 And to love and respect yourself by treating the body you have been given as a temple and the hours of your life as a stewardship from Elohim.

119 Any law that is contrary to this is a law of man, not God. Any man or rabbi, priest, or Caesar who teaches other than this teaches from a place of darkness, not of light.

120 Therefore, I say unto you, even as you know at a glance a true carpet of Tarsus, know also the truth of Elohim by the firm and simple foundation that has been given.

121 Once you have weighed all things in the balance and the truth you hold does not seem wanting, seek out Elohim in quiet prayer and ask in humility to know of a certainty that which seems right to your heart and mind is true.

122 If you ask with a sincere heart and a repentant life, you will feel the power of God move within your heart a sureness of thought confirming that which your mind has found."

123 "Surely these are enlightened words," Gimiel said as the others nodded in agreement.

124 Yeshua admonished them, "You now hold the candle of truth. Hold it high that others may see the light."

125 And turning to Ephres, Yeshua said, "Keep your devotion to God and remember my words; your greatness is still before you."

126 Then bidding farewell to all the men, Yeshua and his family turned and continued their journey north.

127 And Ephres and the other men stood upon the road looking after them until they were no more to be seen.

FIRST SERMON AT GENNESARET

Excerpted from the Oracles of Celestine Light: Vivus: Chapter 23

One day as he walked along the shore of the lake, the crowd began to press him into the water and pleaded with him to speak to them his wisdom.

17 He saw two ships anchored nearby in the lake, for the fishermen were ashore repairing their nets.

18 Yeshua waded out to one of the ships, and Cephas, his disciple, followed him, for it was a vessel of his friend. And they entered onto the ship and moved off near the shore into deeper water.

19 Yeshua sat upon the ship's bench, and facing the crowd nearby, he taught them, saying, "The wealthy often spend their lives striving to gain that which can be quickly taken by Caesar or bandits or made empty and worthless by illness.

20 Even if they hold it safe until the end of their days, their wealth cannot be carried with them to the next life, nor will they have one coin in the eternity to come.

21 I say unto you, be wiser than the rich. Let your days be filled enriching your good character by keeping the commandments of Sinai, not just in deed but also with

a good spirit and happiness with the simple joys of life.

22 Seek out, good friends, not just with common interests of little worth, but with common characters that seek the greater light of Celestine brilliance, and act selflessly to serve one another and those in need.

23 It is your relationships, one with another, that are a true treasure of this life and eternity.

24 Do not judge others, for every hurtful word or action you mete in judgment against others shall be measured against you by Elohim in the hereafter, and it is only Elohim who sees all and knows all, that can fairly judge anyone for their righteousness and propriety.

25 Do not be afraid of those who are different from you in the way they dress or speak or eat or worship God, for all are the spirit children of Elohim and are your brothers and sisters of spirit.

26 Instead, rejoice in the things you have in common and respect their right to differ from you, as they respect your right to differ from them.

27 In the words that I say, think not that I am condoning any evil act contrary to the commandments of Sinai.

28 I merely implore you to not be as the scribes and Pharisees who strain at gnats and swallow camels.

29 If you have devotion to God, show it by loving the temple of your body which Elohim has given you for your sojourn in life.

30 Praising Elohim in your words and songs brings happiness in Heaven, and when you honor the temple you have been given, you honor the gift, and in honoring the gift, you honor the giver.

31 But if you honor not the temple of your body with the purity of the things you eat and drink and with the simple yet elegant beauty of your clothes and adornment, then you trample upon the gift of God that you are and dishonor Elohim with your actions far greater than any praises or pious acts may ever overcome.

32 And beware of what evil your eyes behold, for as your eyes see so your life becomes.

33 Look therefore to surround yourself with virtuous friends. Choose to see things that respect, uplift, and edify you and others and turn your back upon that which does not.

34 In the things that you eat, look beyond that which is clean or unclean and choose that which shows respect for life over that which does not.

35 Eat first those things which have been put upon the earth by Elohim to nourish you without taking their life and those plants which will fade after a season.

36 Consider the olive and the fig trees. They give you wonderful substance that comes again and again without harm to the trees of life. And when you eat their fruits, or the birds or animals eat, they help the trees by carrying their seeds to propagate them.

37 Look at the crops of the fields that are here today and wither tomorrow. They also seek only to make again their kind, and as you plant their seeds, you fulfill them even as they fill you.

38 Nor should you neglect the insects that come numberless as the sands of the sea. Most are not sent to consume your crops, but given to feed you in great abundance. Their lives are short that in them yours may

be long.

39 In these gifts of God, you find the light of life to live long and in health.

40 "But if you need still more, especially because of famine or drought or cold, gather to you the fish that school, for they have been given in great numbers that in them your years upon the earth may be greatly numbered.

41 In the world, there is much darkness among men in the disrespect they have for life in the food they eat.

42 Show by your example the higher path of life. You can fight against the darkness and thereby make enemies of the men of darkness, or you can bring the Celestine Light and the darkness will depart, for it cannot stand to be in the presence of the light.

43 Darkness cannot bear the Celestine Light, and light can always overcome darkness if it stays connected to the source, which is Elohim.

SERMON AT CAPERNAUM

Excerpted from the Oracles of Celestine Light: Vivus: Chapter 24

On the Sabbath of that week, Yeshua went to the synagogue at Capernaum and was given a time to read the scriptures aloud.

2 But he read not a single word from the scrolls. Instead, he taught them with his light, saying, "In the synagogue, much is spoken about the law, much is spoken about keeping the commandments of Sinai, and this is from sincere devotions to Elohim and honest desires to do that which is pleasing to God.

3 But in seeking to be devout, do not be led into the pit of obeying the law but being empty of the spirit and the Celestine Light of Elohim.

4 To obey the law without the spirit is like casting a net for fish on dry land. You are making an effort, but it will gain you only frustration.

5 But the man who casts his net into the lake with vigor, even when done in ignorance as to the proper way to fish or the correct place to cast his net, will still catch fish because of his enthusiasm and effort, even as the man with a true spirit will find the favor of Elohim, while the man who obeys every law without spirit will never know God.

6 So it is in your life. Within the commandments of

Sinai are found all the law Elohim asks of you, save the Great Commandment. Live these simple principles with spirit and you will gain the fullest blessings of Elohim, both in this life and the life to come.

7 Know that all other laws are given by men or added to by men, even if they are read from the scrolls in the synagogue.

8 Decide for yourself with the spirit of God as your guide, which laws serve God and help you have the light of Elohim in your heart, and which serve the Caesars, both the grand and the petty, by keeping you passive and controlled like a flock of sheep."

9 Hearing his teachings, many of those present started murmuring, for this was doctrine such as they had never heard before.

10 But Yeshua continued to instruct them, asking, "Who among you knows the Great Commandment of which I spoke?"

11 Again there was murmuring as they conferred one with another to agree upon the answer to his question. Silias the Elder answered, "It is to marry many wives and bring many children into the world." And there were chuckles and even laughter at his reply.

12 Yeshua said unto them, "You have answered correctly in part, but the response of levity is not in keeping with the weight of this law.

13 Before the commandments of Sinai came the Great Commandment. When this commandment is lived in wholeness and purity, it is a blessing upon the Children of Light. But it is more often lived in perversion, which brings a darkness upon the soul.

14 When the progenitors of man first came upon the earth, Elohim blessed them with the Great Commandment that the righteous might inherit the bounties of earth and Heaven, saying, 'Be fruitful, and multiply; replenish the earth and be good stewards over it.

15 Have sacred dominion over the fish of the sea and over the fowl of the air and over every living thing that moves or grows upon the earth, that in your stewardship, they also might be fruitful and multiply and spread forth over the earth in abundance.'

16 And Elohim said, 'Behold, I have given you every herb bearing seed, which is upon the face of all the earth, and every tree whose seed bears fruit of sweetness or meat, and the milk of the beasts, and the non-fertile eggs of the fowls, and the honey of the bees, and these shall be your food.

17 And to every beast of the earth and to every fowl of the air and to everything that creeps upon the earth, wherein there is life, I have given every green herb from the smallest to the largest, for their meat.'

18 And you will say that these are not the words of the Great Commandment that have been read in the synagogue all of your life, and I say unto you that you have not even lived the portion of the Great Commandment that you have.

19 But now I ask you to be more than you have been and to live the Great Commandment in its fullness that you might receive an inheritance of light in this life and the next.

20 And what is that fullness? Look closely, for there is

much given in the first commandment of God for the children of men.

21 Consider what it means for men and women to multiply and replenish the earth.

22 Obviously, a man cannot do it by himself when we speak of children, but only with a woman may he procreate.

23 Does that then mean that a man or a woman with uncommon affections for their own should be scorned and whipped and even put to death as sometimes occurs among the religious zealots?

24 Why do you think those with uncommon affections are the way they are? Did not Elohim make them so? Will you scorn and whip and put Elohim to death?

25 Unless they were irresistibly compelled by their nature from God to be as they are, do you think they would choose to be reviled and beaten throughout their lives?

26 But if they have uncommon affections one for another, how then can they obey the Great Commandment? In truth, they cannot in the way of a man and a woman create children.

27 But there is far more to the great commandment than bringing new children into the world, for what is missed when those with uncommon affections do not have children is more than compensated by the men and women who have a great abundance of children.

28 The central point of the Great Commandment is not merely to have children, but to be good stewards and multiply and replenish the earth and all life therein, in all aspects, of which children are but one.

29 If two people with uncommon affections have love one for another and sanctify it and are faithful to it within the covenant of marriage and are good stewards of the earth, helping to protect it and all the life therein and helping to increase and magnify it and all life therein, they have fulfilled the Great Commandment far more than the man and the woman who have many children, but are so taxed with so many that they are unable to give them either their time or love or meet their most basic of temporal needs."

30 At this last pronouncement, many stood up, yelling in anger at that which Yeshua taught, and even some of his disciples looked at one another questioningly.

31 Yeshua raised his hands and motioned for everyone to sit down and listen to all he had to say.

32 Then he continued saying, "You see in my words the fulfillment of that which I have said from the beginning. I have not come to uphold the law, but to destroy it, save for the Great Commandment and the true commandments of Sinai, for the laws of Elohim have been perverted by the desires of men.

33 Hear me now. I come not just to destroy, but to bring you a new light far greater than you have known, even the sacred light, Celestine.

34 Before you tear me asunder or turn me over to the persecution of the Romans, hear all that I have to say and weigh my words with the sense of your head and the feeling of your heart.

35 In commanding man to multiply and replenish the earth, Elohim gave men and women a righteous desire for one another and pleasure in fulfilling the desire.

36 But this was countered by the commandments to not commit fornication or adultery. Therefore, only in a bonded relationship, publicly acknowledged in marriage, could a man and woman virtuously fulfill the carnal desire for one another that dwelt within them.

37 Why should men and women not just be like so many of the animals who rut with who they will? The animals' rut, and they are no different after than before. They rut again, and still they change not.

38 Hear me, men and women of Gennesaret. You are spirit sons and daughters of Elohim, of a living Father and Mother in Heaven.

39 Verily, you are here on this earth for more than pleasure and sensual fulfillment. You are here to show God that you can become more than you began and to help others to do likewise.

40 Conquer your lust, keep it virtuous and in your marriage bed where it is sanctified by God.

41 Be a good steward of yourself first, then of the earth and all that is upon it, and Elohim will make you an eternal steward of much more.

42 Unite in the sacred covenant of marriage. Bring forth children, such as you can care for with your time and coin, into the world through love in your marriage bed and teach them by precept and example in the ways of righteousness that they may walk in the light.

43 In this, you are good stewards, helping your children to become more than they began.

44 And you are also a good steward of your own life, for having children helps you to overcome selfishness, one of the most poisonous darts the adversary will

embed in your heart and mind.

45 Children teach you patience; they give you a window to see Heaven; they help your weaknesses to become your strengths.

46 For a man to live his life with a woman and a woman with a man, in devotion to one another, and for them to bear and raise children, sacrificing their time and treasure for the well-being of their children, this is a light that overcomes the darkness of selfishness.

47 And once overcome, dealings with all others become more cordial; criminal acts less common and wars less likely.

48 Righteous marriage with children teaches selflessness and compromise by each individual for the happiness of one another and the good of the family, and these lessons carry forth into the wider world of community and nations.

49 Striving to live a righteous marriage with children forges the weaknesses of men and women into their strengths, even as fornication and adultery or a life without marriage and children brings a forgetfulness of the light and opens the transgressor to greater susceptibility to further darkness.

50 These principals of light are so important and needful for expansion of the light within you that the man and woman who are barren should always adopt children who are without parents, so both may be filled with the love and growth that only a parent and child can bring to one another.

51 Consider again now the men who have affections for men and the women who have affections for women.

52 Elohim made them as they are, by their request, before they were born of woman, that they might have the opportunity in life to be sorely tested and grow great in stature as they overcome their challenges, but also that they might more easily embody the balance of male and female that can lead to becoming a living testament of the Celestine Light.

53 Do you think then that Elohim would condemn them for the nature that was given to them and disdain their righteous desire to have greater burdens and greater potential for reward any more than the fish would be condemned for swimming or the bird for flying?

54 But there is a trap laid for them of selfishness, and many are those that are caught by it, for as they are scorned and cast away from those who rebuke them, they may be enticed into their lusts and begin to live for their lust and pleasure and comfort, thus are led step by step down the path to damnation instead of the exaltation they sought.

55 I say unto you, do not, by your actions of condemnation, encourage them down that path.

56 Verily, there are many alternatives within the Great Commandment, and if they accept a stewardship of the earth and the life therein and fulfill it, they have lived the Great Commandment as fully as any husband and wife who cared well for their children.

57 Like with children, fulfilling a stewardship to the earth and all the life therein requires a continued and prolonged sacrifice of your time and your treasure. And in this, you overcome selfishness and become far greater

than you were.

58 Therefore, I say clearly unto you: It is not a sin for a man to have affections for a man or a woman for a woman, if it comes not from carnal lust, but from virtuous love, for such was not forbidden by Elohim in the Great Commandment or the commandments of Sinai.

59 But with those who love their own kind, let them lust not after one another into fornication, but remain virtuous and only have intimacy within the bonds of marriage, even as it is for a man and a woman.

60 But there are also differences that must be respected. Where a man may have two or more wives and they may love one another even as they love their husband, let there be no other men but two in a marriage with one another, for beyond this men are given to purely carnal lusts over love.

61 Let all marriages be in public. Let the unmarried keep their chastity before marriage and guard their virtue zealously once married.

62 And I say unto you, let any who would commit fornication before marriage or adultery after marriage suffer the full weight of their transgression before man and God until they have repented and asked forgiveness and made restitution to all they have wronged."

63 Again there arose a great hue and cry and much consternation among the people in the temple at the words of Yeshua, for never had they heard anything similar to what he had said unto them, and it was vastly different from all they had ever been taught.

64 Yet they were astonished at his doctrine and the

power of his words, and despite their shock at his teachings, many were not as angry as they supposed they should have been and some found themselves nodding in agreement, for his teachings made sense in their heads and resonated in their hearts.

65 Then a man stood up and yelled, "You are a false teacher! You would undermine the sanctity of our homes and marriages with your words of perversion. Truly, evil must dwell within you to say such things."

66 Yeshua answered him, saying, "It is your actions to put aside and persecute those who are not like you that weakens the fabric of your home and marriage, for cast away and reviled, they are more likely to be angry and revengeful and fall onto the paths of lust and fornication, as the path of virtue and honor is forbidden by those who condemn them.

67 Let each be as they were created within the boundaries of a righteous marriage, given the opportunity to be good stewards and live lives of virtue and honor, and your home and marriage will be far more protected."

68 Then Yeshua spoke commandingly, pointing into the crowd, "That you may see the truth that I am the light and not be offended by my teachings, but uplifted, bring that man to me."

69 Now the man he spoke of had glared at him in silence through all he had said. But when everyone looked at him because Yeshua pointed to him, his face contorted in rage and he growled like a wild animal.

70 He turned to quickly depart, but Yeshua spoke forcibly to him, saying, "Turn and face the Celestine

Light, demon of darkness."

71 The man turned to face Yeshua, drool now coming from his mouth, his face twisted in anger, and his voice garbled and growling, and said, "Let me alone! What have I to do with you, Yeshua of Nazareth? Have you come to destroy me? I know who you are, Holy Son of Elohim. Leave me be!"

72 Yeshua commanded, "Speak no more! Depart this instant! Let the light near every darkness thwart you to ever again dwell in man."

73 The man fell to the floor with a piercing scream and began to thrash about for a few seconds, and then he was still.

74 Slowly, he opened his eyes and, gingerly feeling his body, found that he was unhurt. And his face, which was full of dirt, shone with a countenance of light.

75 All who witnessed it were amazed. And the men and women in the synagogue spoke among themselves, saying, "What power is this? What can this new doctrine be, for with authority and power even the unclean spirits obey him and depart at his command?"

76 As the people departed the synagogue, they separated hurriedly each to their own path, anxious to tell their friends everything they had seen and heard. And Yeshua's fame soon spread throughout all the region of Galilee.

77 After leaving the synagogue, Yeshua and Miriam went with Cephas and Amram to Cephas' home in Bethsaida, and Ya'akov and Yohhanan went with them.

78 Upon arriving, they found that the mother of Cephas was sick with a great fever.

79 Yeshua came and held his hands above her body for a moment, moving them slightly, with his eyes closed as if in silent prayer.

80 Then laying his hands upon her head, he rebuked the fever and took her by the hand, lifting her up from her bed.

81 She arose well and whole with a great smile and words of gratitude and immediately went to the string hanging from the ceiling and brought dates out for them to eat.

82 In the evening, as the sun set, many of the people of the town came to the house of Cephas, for everyone had heard of the earlier events at the synagogue and they desired to see and hear Yeshua.

83 They brought many who were diseased and others who were possessed of devils to Yeshua.

84 And those who were diseased and attested in sincerity to repent of their sins and walk in the light, he healed of many diverse sicknesses.

85 But he rebuked those who would not repent in sincerity, saying, "Only the pure in heart can be healed by the Celestine Light of Elohim.

86 Repent first of your sins that the light may find a place in you. When the light is in your heart, all things are possible."

87 From five men and two women, he cast out demons, but he did not allow the demons to speak, because he did not want them to say who he was as the demon in the synagogue had. The darkness unmistakably knew the light, but the common people were not yet prepared to receive this knowledge.

88 From this day forth, a Community of Light began to form in the region of the three towns of the delta on Lake Gennesaret.

89 And in the weeks to come, many were baptized by the disciples called by Yeshua, and when they came out of the water, in their hearts was a light brighter than the sun.

SERMON AT SYCTHOPOLIS

Excerpted from the Oracles of Celestine Light: Vivus: Chapter 25

During the following months, Yeshua traveled all through Galilee and into Syria and Judea, teaching the Gospel of Celestine Light in the synagogues and in the open-air temples of Elohim.

2 In each town and village, he healed the sick and diseased who were pure in heart and came to him with a contrite spirit.

3 Miriam and his disciples baptized many who had heard his words and felt the spirit of Elohim moving in their hearts, and they rose from the water and were called Children of Light.

4 Those who were baptized showed the truth of their convictions by repenting of their sins and covenanting before man and God to henceforth live in the light.

5 The fame of Yeshua went all throughout Galilee and Syria, and many people with sicknesses and diverse diseases, and torments of the mind and heart, and those possessed with devils and those that had palsy were brought to him; and he healed all of them who were pure in heart.

6 And it came to pass that large crowds began to follow him, and people came from Galilee, from Decapolis and Jerusalem and Judea, and from Perea and lands beyond

the Jordan.

7 One morning, while encamped near Sycthopolis, Yeshua arose well before dawn and went out to a solitary place toward the mountain, west of the town, and prayed there.

8 When Miriam and the disciples awoke, the disciples wondered where he was, and Miriam told them and they went to him.

9 When they found him, alone on a hillside, Cephas asked, "A great crowd looks for you this morning. When shall I tell them that you will come?"

10 Yeshua began walking back down the hill as he answered Cephas, saying, "I will come now and speak to those who are here this morning. Then let us go into the next towns that I may preach and you may baptize, for that is why we are here in this moment."

11 Coming down to the people waiting for him on the outskirts of the city, Yeshua said unto them, "When you pray, do not pray to an unseen God without a body or form.

12 Know that you are truly children of a Heavenly Mother and Father, and they are as real and tangible as I am.

13 When you pray to them, do not just let words flow out of your mouth, nor repeat each day the same thing you said the previous day.

14 Speak your prayers aloud when you are in a private place, but only in your thoughts when you are in public, unless you have been called upon to stand and pray as a representative for your brothers and sisters of spirit for something which you all desire.

15 In all prayers, before you say a word, take a deep breath and slowly let it out, then another and another, until you are in a quiet place of peace in your heart.

16 Then let your spirit expand beyond your body until you feel one with the grass and the waters and the birds and all life around you.

17 Then expand into the sun and the stars and feel the spirit of Elohim moving in your heart and feel oneness with God in all that you are.

18 When you then pray, speak not to the ethers, nor to a rock, or to the wall in your home, but to the spirit of your heavenly parents which dwells within you, which you are one with in your heart.

19 In humility, bow your head, then raise it up with closed eyes to the sun in your prayers, for all light comes from God, both the spiritual and the physical, and when your eyes are upon the light, it is easier to feel the spirit of Elohim moving in your heart and hear the voice of Elohim speaking in your thoughts.

20 Be a thankful son or daughter of God, for you have been given a life on a most blessed world where food grows of its own accord and beauty and life abounds and surrounds you wherever you look.

21 When you are in the sacred place of prayer in your heart, ask of Elohim any selfless and worthy desire, beyond that which you can do for yourself, and the means for it to come to pass shall be given to you.

22 But ask not for worldly things; save it be with selflessness; only for help with your simple needs and for the good of others and the glory of God.

23 Elohim is not like a distant rich relative to be called

upon to grant your temporal wishes, but a true parent who teaches you good principles that you may prosper on your own, both spiritually and temporally.

24 Verily, your heavenly parents greatly desire your continual well-being and spiritual fulfillment upon earth and your eternal happiness and progression in Heaven.

25 Know that you have been blessed by your heavenly parents with great gifts when you were born to help you in your journey in life.

26 With your talents and listening to your inner light, you can gain all that you seek in the world that is worthy of a son or daughter of God.

27 Not by wishing it were so, but by using the gifts you have been given with prudence and diligence."

28 Then a man named Zuriel asked, "The previous moon, my fishing boat was overcome by a storm and sank into the sea. Now it is hard for my family, for I cannot earn as much working for another as I can for myself. I have asked God for another boat, but you say I should not pray for such things. How then may I get a new boat, for I cannot pay for one on my own?"

29 Yeshua answered him, "You may certainly ask Elohim to help you acquire another boat as it is not for you alone that you ask, but for the good of your family; and you do not ask for an excess, but merely to fulfill your humble needs.

30 But do not expect a new boat to magically appear the next morning at your door, for Elohim helps you with inspiration and ideas and by guiding the answers, the people, and the situations and materials you need,

to help manifest your prayer. Then it is in your hands to use the gifts of Elohim along with your own gifts and talents to help yourself.

31 Have you used your talents and done all that you can do?"

32 Zuriel rubbed his chin as he considered the words of Yeshua and answered, "In truth, I have not. Even as we speak, I have thought of a way I can acquire a boat that I had not considered before and realized that I have spent more time lamenting my misfortune than doing things within my power to remedy it.

33 I will act now in earnestness and call upon God to lend favor to my actions."

34 Yeshua smiled saying, "And so shall your worthy desires and prayers be fulfilled."

35 Then Yeshua continued with his sermon, saying, "Remember, Elohim is the essence of love and light, while the adversary within and the minions of evil spew forth hatred, violence, and darkness.

36 Therefore, let every action of the righteous man or woman always be one of light and life and love, and you shall ever have the spirit of Elohim as your constant companion to lift your spirit and surround you in the light you seek, and the adversary shall have no place within you.

37 With the Celestine Light of Elohim in your heart and guiding your thoughts and actions, you will find contentment in simple things and success in your selfless endeavors, both great and small.

38 If you choose your actions based upon the good that will be gained for others by accomplishing your

tasks, you will always find the favor of Elohim to help you in your desires.

39 That is not to say that you cannot also gain, but that he who seeks only for himself has no favor from God and no friends upon the earth, while he who seeks righteous things of which others may also freely benefit shall be blessed by Elohim and honored in sincerity by men."

40 Then Yeshua beckoned for the sick and afflicted to come to him, and the repentant and pure in heart, he healed, every one.

41 When he made ready to depart to another city, the people asked him to stay with them and were greatly desirous that he should not depart from them.

42 But with love, he said unto them, "It must needs be that I also preach across the land that others might see the true Celestine Light of Elohim and repent and be healed both inside and out; that they might be a light of God among men even as the good people of Sycthopolis."

43 And though they were sad at his departure, they understood his words and, with thankfulness, asked that he would return again to them soon.

44 But some could not bear to see him leave, and they followed after him.

FIRST SERMON AT PTOLEMAIS

Excerpted from the Oracles of Celestine Light: Vivus: Chapter 26

From Sycthopolis, Yeshua and Miriam and the disciples returned to Nazareth for a night, and then journeyed to Ptolemais on the coast, where Yeshua had gone sometimes during his youth to meditate while looking over the sea and to mingle with the many foreigners in the city.

2 As they traveled, Miriam walked with him, and one time when the others were trailing far behind, she asked, "My Lord, when shall you reveal the greater secrets of the Celestine Light to the disciples you have called to follow you?"

3 Yeshua answered her, saying, "They are still like babes upon their mother's breast. They must continue with milk before they can tolerate the substance of that which is greater. And there are others I must call, and there must be a Quorum of Twelve before I will speak of the fullness of the Celestine Light to them.

4 Many things I shall not tell them until the very last days before I depart from the world. And many things will wait for you to reveal to them once I have returned to my Father and Mother in Heaven."

5 Miriam protested, saying, "My dear husband, you know they only tolerate me because I am your wife.

When you are gone, I fear I shall have no standing with them and they will not heed my words, nor do I wish to even be upon the earth if you are not here with me."

6 Yeshua held her hand as they walked and kissed her lightly on the cheek, saying, "Though my body may be gone, my spirit will never leave you, and the substance of my essence will be so strong with you that it will be as if I walk beside you still.

7 It must needs be that you remain for a time after I have returned from whence I came to nurture our children and the flame of Celestine Light, for before a night has passed ere I have left the earth, there will be many who will begin to pervert my teachings.

8 Even among my elect who hold fast to my light, there will be some who will not be able to overcome their own weaknesses and will heed you not.

9 Then will come those who never knew me, but act in my name, calling themselves my Apostles and bishops. And they will have a fanatic zeal to purge all of your words, even the record of your life from the annals of men.

10 Such as these are not worthy for the higher Celestine Light that you will offer. But those who are worthy, though their numbers will be small, will receive you with love, honor, and humility. And as marvelous as you are, the Miriam they will know then will be far more than the Miriam they know today."

11 That evening they slept outside the walls of the city, and as the sun rose, they entered through the east gate.

12 Yeshua sent his disciples to go into the markets, along the quays and into the streets, proclaiming his

coming.

13 The disciples were diligent in their task, and many people came the following day to hear Yeshua speak during their midday break.

14 Many were interested because the disciples told them how Yeshua did not teach the same teachings of old they had heard before, but shared how to have a better life and know God as a friend.

15 And it came to pass that over four hundred people gathered at the synagogue where Yeshua had come, and he blessed them for seeking a greater light and said unto them, "Though you may have a comfortable home and a work that pays you well, if you do not have the spirit of Elohim in your heart, which is evident by your actions of kindness, selflessness, generosity, and love, you have nothing.

16 For the things of this world are here today and gone tomorrow, but the spirit of Elohim abiding in your heart and manifested in your actions gives a comfort in life that all the money of the world cannot buy and a palace in eternity greater than any Caesar can imagine.

17 Though you may think you are young and have good health, if you do not live as God has given for you to live in the food you eat and that which you drink and in the way you love the temple of your body which Elohim has built, then your end is misery in life and wretched remorse for what could have been in the world to come.

18 You have heard it said from the prophets of old that the people of ancient days lived for hundreds of years, even Methuselah, the son of Enoch, who lived for 969

years. How is it then that you know not one person who has reached one hundred years and will count yourself blessed if you live to fifty years?

19 Were the people more righteous than you in the days before? Nay, most were not, for the scriptures are ripe with the accounts of their unrighteousness.

20 But there were some who walked closer to the ways of Elohim, and they reaped many blessings, which included a long and fruitful life.

21 Think not that I speak of the law, for most of the law is of men and I have come to destroy it, not honor it.

22 But if you remember that you are a temple built by Elohim and have been given to live upon a paradise created by Elohim and you honor your temple and partake of your Eden in righteousness and respect, then all that the righteous ancients had shall be yours as well.

23 Your Eden was given to be breathed in purity, and in such your body is renewed by the very air. Therefore, do not breathe the smoke of fires or even a candle lest you destroy the renewal God has blessed you with. And let the barbaric practice of breathing the smoke of herbs to ward off evil spirits have no place in your life or within the walls of your home, for the smoke of anything is death, not life.

24 Elohim has charged you to be a steward over every living thing and over all the earth, all of which are given for your benefit and as you have need.

25 As a good steward, you must respect your charges and never despoil a land no matter how small, without restoring it to its splendor, nor take a life no matter how insignificant, save there is no other way to sustain or

protect your own.

26 Therefore, do not kill the animals or the birds to eat their flesh, for they love their life, even as you love yours.

27 Choose whenever possible to eat only those things of life that Elohim has put in your Eden to give you sustenance without taking life that would have continued for years.

28 Therefore, first eat the fruits of the trees and bushes that give you freely of their pulp that you might spread their seeds and propagate their kind.

29 If you still hunger, eat of the vegetables that give you their fruit and of the plants that wither and die each year and were therefore given to be consumed.

30 But cook them not, for then you have sustenance without life, and each bite brings you closer to your own death. Heat them only enough to enhance the life, not extinguish it.

31 If because of drought or famine or your situation at the time, you cannot be strengthened from plants alone, then eat the lower forms of life: the insects and the schooling fish of the sea.

32 And all others, you should never eat, save it be that there is no other way to save your life at the time.

33 Remember well my words. The more you eat that which still has life and is given freely without fight or resistance, the more you will be renewed to live beyond the years of men in health and wisdom.

34 Use this simple test: If the meal you desire that lives free would try to escape from you and not go meekly and quietly to your plate if it knew your intentions, then

it is a life you should spare unless you have no other way to sustain your own.

35 If you domesticate animals to help you with your tasks and treat them with respect as a good steward, Elohim will show you favor. But do not eat for food those creatures which have pleasure in the company of their friends, for they are like you, only in a different kind of body, and eating them would be the same as eating your best friend.

36 Though you might have sustenance in the moment, the despair the animal you slew felt in death taints the meat with a toxin of death that brings you closer to your own grave with each bite.

37 Consider now the sun in the sky that brings you warmth and light each day. This is the very essence of Elohim, and as such its power is greater than you can imagine. It can give you life or death depending upon your wisdom.

38 Each day, you should come into the light of the sun. Let it shine into your closed eyes; feel its warmth upon your bare skin, for this very light of Elohim purifies your body inside and out.

39 But be wise and do not linger too long lest you get burned like the bread left too long in the oven, making that which was good become bad.

40 Consider also the water that you drink. Let it be pure without the waste of people or animals, for your body is an ocean and if you keep your water clear, your ocean will still have life long after your friends who heeded not my words have dried up and blown away with the wind.

41 Nor should water just be to drink but also to keep your body clean, and I speak not just of your hands and feet and mouth. Cleaning only those is like only cleaning the doorways of the synagogue. If you love your temple, clean all of it each day. As you care for your temple, so it shall care for you.

42 Nor should you be slothful in the use of your body. Elohim did not create your temple with all its moving parts for you to lounge around on couches, eating grapes as the Romans do.

43 Each day, consider how you can move all parts of your temples in a myriad of ways. Stretch them, strain them, challenge them, and they will become stronger and bring you health and longevity.

44 Take the path of ease and you will have comfort in the moment, but the total of your moments will be far less upon the world.

45 What of your habits? Have you considered how your traits and the way you treat yourself and others might be a great weight upon the scale of your health, life, and happiness?

46 Your actions begin with your thoughts, and if these are not pure, neither will be the actions that follow.

47 What then is a pure thought? Does that mean you cannot lust for your wife? No, it does not, for lust for your wife with love is of God, but lust for another man's wife is impure and will shorten your days upon the earth and lessen your reward in Heaven, even if you never act upon your thought.

48 If you say a mean and spiteful thing to your brother or sister, it will eat like a sickness in your heart and take

away the days of your life. Even if you only think an evil thought of your brother or sister, but say it not, it will still be a sickness inside that consumes you.

49 Therefore, be not easily offended by the actions of others, whether they are your brother or sister, father or mother, children or friends. Be quick to smile and laugh and slow to condemn or judge and your years upon the earth will be greatly multiplied, and each one will be a treasure.

50 If you would have the happiness of a new bride and the age of the ancients, then let your greatest habit be love. Let each thought and breath be an expression of greater love, not just for your family, but for your friends and your acquaintances and even your enemies.

51 For Elohim loves you with a love greater than the sun, despite your weaknesses.

52 Love is the greatest fountain of life you will ever know. Therefore, let it flow from you in abundance by your thoughts and words and actions.

53 And by this, your enemies will become your friends and your friends will honor you, and your family shall cherish you, and your life will be long and full of great joy.

54 And if you love your family and friends, you will be a good steward and serve them and help them in their lives. In this, you also serve yourself, for in every good deed you do, Elohim adds to your days of joy upon the earth.

55 Lastly, remember to have a good balance in your life.

56 Many people and duties call to you and are in need

of your time. Give to all with equality, but do not neglect your own needs for contemplation and prayer and rest.

57 Your temple needs proper amounts of good food and water and air and movement. Therefore, take heed to have balance each day in these things.

58 Take heed to consider the merits of all points of view and do not pass judgment upon others simply because they are not like you, for all are children of your Father and Mother in Heaven.

59 Never forget that Elohim has taken a portion of Heaven and put it upon the earth to be your Eden that you might live long upon the land and prosper. And so it shall be if you live your life worthy of the gifts you have been given."

60 Then Yeshua was quiet for a moment so that his words might move within the hearts of the people. And in the eyes of some, a new light dawned, but in others, their countenance was dark for they could not abide the things Yeshua had said, which for them were not as they were inclined to live.

61 Yeshua, perceiving the thoughts of the people, said unto them, "There once was a noble man who owned much land and hired many men.

62 The Lord was a good steward over the lands and people that had been given to his dominion, and he continually looked for ways to reward his faithful workmen and to give them greater responsibilities and stewardship that they might become more than they began.

63 And it came to pass that there was one young man he greatly favored, for he had a willing heart and a quick

mind.

64 Therefore, one day the Lord said to his worker, 'Today is the day of your fulfillment. You have worked diligently and faithfully for me, and now I shall make you master of my mill and of the men who work there. It shall all be in your charge.'

65 The man was very grateful for his reward and worked even more diligently than before. He kept the mill clean and organized the work to be more efficient so that soon they were producing more flour than the mill had ever produced before, and the Lord was pleased.

66 Three years passed and the mill continued to prosper under the stewardship of the mill master, but despite his greater wealth, the man seemed to age far more than three years.

67 The Lord was concerned for him, so he went in secret to inquire in his village about the man, for he favored him and worried that he might be in some trouble.

68 In the village, he was told that since he had become master of the mill, the man thought only of his work. He neglected his wife and children. He slept little, and he came home later than all others and drank far too much wine every night.

69 Straightaway the next morning, the Lord called his mill master to him and spoke of the things he had learned. And the mill master answered, 'It is true, my Lord. I have neglected my wife and children, because I have served you first as I knew I must.

70 It is difficult to run a mill well, for there are many things to deal with each day. When I come home, I am

tired, and the wine has helped me to sleep quickly so I can be prepared to arise early and serve you again the next day.

71 Please do not be angry with me for I have only wanted to serve you well. I have been saddened to see what has become of my personal life, but I have willingly given up some pleasures that I can have others that more money can buy, that my children can have more than I had as a child.'

72 The Lord, seeing the man's good heart, could not be angry with him, but he said unto him, 'You have served me well, and in that I am pleased. But if in the course of your service you destroy your own life, you will steal from me the many hours of good work I could have otherwise had from you if you had cared as much for yourself and your family as you do for your work.

73 I did not ask you to lose your life because of me, but gave you your reward that you and your family might have a better life.

74 Understand, it is not from money or position that happiness comes, but from being a good steward over all that is in your charge.'

75 The mill master was confused, saying, 'My Lord, you must know that I am a good steward. The mill has never produced as much as it does under my care.'

76 And the Lord answered, 'I speak not of the mill for that is but one board in the wheel of your life. It is of the other boards that I speak and of the hub.

77 Your wife is a part of your wheel of great importance, and you must take the time to love her and be with her.

78 The mill can be destroyed tomorrow and it can be

rebuilt, but if you destroy the love of your wife because of your neglect, it will be much more difficult to rebuild that which was lost.

79 Each of your children are also parts of your wheel, and whether they will grow strong and delightful depends upon your presence and love and example of virtue.

80 They are children for only a precious few years. If you do not cherish every moment with them and seek out time to share with them, then the sun will set on your time together and will never rise again, for they will be children no more.

81 And your family and friends are also parts of the vitality of the wheel of your life. If you neglect them and do not listen to their problems and help them in their needs, they will turn away from you, and in your time of need, your wheel will fail for lack of support.

82 Lastly, my good mill master, you are the hub of your wheel. If you drink too much and sleep too little, if you eat poorly and do not take time to reflect and contemplate and commune with God, then your hub will become bound and you will be seized.

83 Your journey will end before its time because you were not a good steward over the things that were actually the most important.

84 If you can be such a wonderful mill master and such a good steward over the things which I have given to you, then can you not be an even greater steward over that which God has given unto you, even your very life and your wife and your children and family and friends?'

85 And the mill master fell to his knees in tears, for the truth of the Lord's words had been like a spear into his heart. And he cried out, 'Lord, forgive me for being a steward more over that which was least and not enough over that which was greater.

86 Give me another chance and I will be the good and faithful steward you have shown me I should be.'

87 The Lord was well pleased. He raised the mill master from his knees and bid him go home, saying, 'I will see you at the mill tomorrow, but today I think your greater stewardship beckons.'

88 Quickly, the man returned to his wife and children, and there was great joy in their house thereafter.

89 I say unto you, be like the mill master; remember that being a good steward is pleasing to God, but it begins with honoring and caring for the temple of your own body that Elohim has given to you and then by loving your wife and nurturing your children with your time and sincere attention.

90 Verily, it matters not what success you have in the world. If you fail to care for the vessel God has given you, if you fail to give ample love and time to your wife and children, then all else you do is for naught, for your life will be unhappiness and your eternity will be emptiness.

91 But do not despair; for you are children of God, you are Children of Light. Remember who you are, let your heart go to Elohim, and it will always guide you to happiness in this life and fulfillment in eternity."

SECOND SERMON IN PTOLEMAIS

Excerpted from the Oracles of Celestine Light: Vivus: Chapter 27

The following day, Yeshua again gave a sermon during the midday rest, and the number of people who came to hear him was greater than the previous day, numbering over six hundred, including men, women, and children.

2 Many people came early and brought food and drink with them so they could listen to his preaching while they ate their midday meal. And numerous small awnings were set up in the crowd to shade the young and old from the sun.

3 Ptolemais was a bustling city with residents and visitors from all parts of the Mediterranean and beyond. Among those who came to hear Yeshua were both the rich and the poor, Hebrews of many persuasions and Gentiles of many lands, including a number of Romans. It was with this varied audience in mind that Yeshua chose the subjects of his sermon.

4 And Yeshua said unto them, "Is Elohim the God of the life to come or the God of the life you live?

5 Truly, Elohim is the God of both. Yet how different is the life you live from the life you expect to live in the

hereafter?

6 Your life in mortality is meant to be a challenge that you may grow stronger and of more sure faith. But it is not meant to be misery, for the man who is beat down without end eventually becomes so numb from torment that he stops trying to rise to something better.

7 It is for this cause that those who unnecessarily cause pain and suffering in others, giving pain and suffering instead of compassion, will reap the evil that they sowed, seventy times seventy in the hereafter after they are weighed in the balance and found wanting.

8 So too will the man or woman who gives compassion instead of torment reap their good reward in the hereafter, seventy times seventy after they are weighed in the balance and found to have multiplied their light.

9 Nevertheless, though you may die in a moment, the hereafter seems distant and far away, even but a dream, while your challenges of today are unavoidably before you, both those you inflict upon yourself and those inflicted upon you by others.

10 But you are the master of the Celestine Light that dwells within you. If you choose to embrace the light, there is no darkness deep enough to overcome you.

11 If you choose to let the Celestine Light of Elohim fill your body, no problems in life are great enough to take away the warmth and tranquility you will feel inside.

12 Though you may be poor, you will feel rich.

13 Though you may be persecuted, you will feel peace, without anxiety.

14 Though you may hunger even for food, you will

feel filled.

15 Think not that Elohim is the God only of the world to come, for it is Elohim that made the world you now live upon and everything in it, and this for your happiness, joy, and fulfillment.

16 Life becomes sour for many people only because they do not take good actions to make it sweet like honey; therefore, it spoils and becomes unpalatable.

17 Verily, I say unto you that Elohim gave you a world where life abounds that your life might have exceeding joy by being one in spirit with all the life around you.

18 Go and stare for an hour at the sea, listening to the waves lapping on the beach. Rest in your garden for an hour and quietly watch the bees gathering nectar on the flowers or the ants patiently building their nest by removing one small grain of sand at a time.

19 Take time to immerse yourself often, if only for an hour or a day, in the life of the world around you, and you will find the Celestine Light of Elohim comes alive inside of you, and your burdens become lighter and your life becomes brighter.

20 When a man becomes a man, he stops being like a child and he thinks well of himself. But in truth, when a man stops being like a child and takes life too seriously, it becomes drudgery and monotony, and his life goes from the continual pure happiness of a child to the frequent unhappiness of a man.

21 The more years of drudgery and monotony that pass, the more unhappiness builds within the man, until in his old age he becomes as shriveled as a stale dried date, with little of the soft joy remaining from his

youth.

22 Does this sound like anyone you know? Perhaps even you? Have you become so caught up in being an adult that you have forgotten how to be a child?

23 Do you play with your own children, sharing in their delight at a new discovery or accomplishment?

24 You may say that you have no time for the foolishness of children. But I say unto you there is little that is as great of importance, for unless a man can easily and often become as a little child, he can in no way enter into the glory of the Kingdom of Heaven.

25 Being as a child does not throw off your responsibilities as an adult. It merely seeks a balance of stewardship to your family and stewardship to yourself of recognizing that there is a time to work and a time to play, and that the time to play, just like the time to work, comes every day, except for the Sabbath.

26 For this cause look often for occasions to celebrate. At the end of each week of work, reward yourself and your family with a special celebration, even if it is only an extra date for a dessert and a quiet hour on the beach with your family.

27 Celebrate the planting even if you are not a farmer, for you still hope for fair weather and a good crop that you may have food on your table.

28 For the same reason, celebrate the harvest; whether the bounty came from the farmers' fields or your own plot of land, it is the blessing of life and the pleasure of good food.

29 Celebrate each full moon, even if your life has been greatly challenged during that moon, for you still live

and still enjoy great blessings.

30 If the lamp of Elohim is lit inside of you, then you will always see the blessings that surround you. Your joys will be magnified in your heart, and your sorrows lessened.

31 Celebrate each birthday in your family, even if only with an orange and a day off from work, for each soul of life is a blessing, and each step you walk in life is laying the foundation for your eternity.

32 As you celebrate the lives of your loved ones, your thoughtfulness reminds them of how special they are to you, even as they will remember how wonderful you are to them.

33 As a community, look for occasions to be festive and celebrate things great and small, for sharing and rejoicing together is the glue that binds the stew pot of cultures and people, that is, Ptolemais.

34 Why do you think I speak to you of these things? It is to help you to know that God did not create you to have endless sorrow, but to have endless joy.

35 You were not born to wait for death as a blessing, merely hoping to escape life and pass to an eternal paradise. Verily, God gave you life and gave you this world that you would have joy and make it into a paradise, beginning within the walls of your own home.

36 You may be accustomed to hearing a long list of laws you must obey from your priests, but the only laws I give you today are to acknowledge God in all things and to treat your neighbor in your thoughts, words, and deeds as you would hope to be treated by them.

37 Respect and humility toward God and respect and

courtesy to your neighbors are the foundations of peace on earth and everlasting joy in Heaven.

38 But what does that mean to you who live in Ptolemais? Here your neighbor may be a Roman or a Persian or a Syrian or a Greek, all with beliefs and habits different than yours and perhaps even objectionable. Is this a cause to fight with your neighbor or just to disdain them?

39 I say unto you, do not fight them or disdain them, but accept them and respect them if they are of good character."

40 Then Yeshua pointed to a man with a red sash far to his right at the edge of the crowd and another with a brown sash far to his left and beckoned them to stand, and he said, "Though Elohim is the one God of all the earth and every star in the sky, there are many ways to find and know God, even as those who sit to my right see me differently than those who sit to my left; yet both see me.

41 If I were to ask these two men to come to me, they could not walk in each other's footsteps. In truth, they would have to take very different paths. Yet both would have their eyes upon me, both would be seeking me, and in the end, I would embrace them both as they came to me.

42 Therefore, do not look to see if a person is from the same country as you or the same faith to befriend them. But look to their good character and virtue as a sure foundation worthy of friendship.

43 If they are seeking God with virtue and good character, even on a path different than yours, know

with certainty that they are loved by Elohim. And if they are loved by Elohim, can you treat them any less?

44 And I say unto you that the day shall come in your lifetime when there shall be contentions among those who live in Ptolemais, and among the narrow-minded, there will be some who will incite violence against those that are not of their tribe or country or faith.

45 On that day, remember my words. If you would show devotion to God, then give only peace and solace and refuge to everyone who has virtue and good character, even as they would return it to you, regardless of the color of their skin, the language they speak, or the path they walk to God.

46 On that day, turn your back upon the instigators of intolerance; support them not. For in the eyes of Elohim, it is far better to give comfort to a man who walks a different path than you, but walks toward God with humility, honesty, and virtue than to stand against such a man and is far worse to stand with the ignorant and intolerant, simply because they are of your faith, or speak your tongue, or are from your tribe.

47 The fact that you listened to the spirit of Elohim that led you here today testifies that you are seeking something greater than you are and are seeking to become more than you have been, not in the ways of the world, but in the ways of God.

48 Remember now my words and the twelve pillars of the Temple of Forever and the capstone over all, which I give to you now in my love for you.

49 The true temple of Elohim is in a circle and no other shape, for only in a circle are all good things included in

harmony and unity.

50 Though man may build a likeness to fulfill his needs for sanctuary and communion on earth, the true temple of Elohim is not built by man, but is within man, as he lives in harmony with the spirit of God.

51 Live these pillars; rest your thoughts and your words and your deeds upon them, and they will support you in life against all that the world may bring upon you and lift you to the highest mountain in the eternity to come.

52 These are among the things God does for you, and you should do no less for yourself and your fellow men.

53 When a choice is to be made between conflict and peace . . . choose peace. Be ever willing to find the path of harmony and common ground and ever reluctant to walk down the path of discord and anger because of differences.

54 There are many pious people who consider themselves godly, but do not act in ways that are pleasing to God; who become angry when others do not walk the same path to God that they do. But I say unto you that a faith that is worthy of God is not based only upon what you believe, but even more upon that which you do.

55 Your actions are the gold of your life, which is weighed in the balance of the scale of Judgment of Resonance. And in the world to come, it will not be asked of you what you believed in life, but rather what did you do in life?

56 Therefore, do unto others as you would have them do unto you; for that which you do to others, both the

good and the bad, will come back and in an equal way to you from others, both in this life and the next.

57 And when good is done to you, reciprocate it back twofold.

58 But when evil is done to you, find forgiveness in your heart; and unto the repentant, do not hesitate to forgive them in your words and your actions.

59 Laugh and play and listen and watch and wonder; be a child each day, for it is one of the secrets of perpetual joy and communion with God, and for this cause have you been created and given this world; that you might have joy in abundance.

60 Be a good steward of all that is in your care by protecting, increasing, and enhancing all that has been entrusted to you, beginning with your own life, then your family, then your brothers and sisters of light, then your community, then your world and the life of everything therein.

61 Verily, the more you serve others, the greater grows your own spirit and stature.

62 Seek knowledge every day; for ignorance is slavery and knowledge is freedom; and these enliven your soul.

63 Verily, it is easier for a man or a woman with knowledge and freedom to do good in the world than one existing in ignorance and slavery.

64 Embrace love as a star to guide your life, for more miracles are possible with love than any other power save faith. In truth, these two work together, and one without the other is but an empty cup.

65 Love yourself first, in humility and truth, for only then can you give true love to others. Such is the circle

of love.

66 Love your wife or husband as you would like them to love you, for when the love within a marriage is returned, it blossoms into a fulfillment and tranquility that is equaled only by the spirit of God flowing in your heart. Such is the circle of love.

67 Love your children as the most precious jewels and show your love by giving them your time each day, which speaks more powerfully of love to them than anything you can say, and it will be returned to you multiplied many times when you are old. Such is the circle of love.

68 Love your brothers and sisters of light and remember you are all part of the family of light; therefore, their concerns are yours, and their joys should be in your heart as well.

69 Care for them in their times of need, even as they will care for you. Such is the circle of love.

70 Love your neighbors, even those who are different from you. Verily, you are all still children of God and brothers and sisters of spirit. An injury to one is an injury to all, and a blessing to one is a blessing to all. Such is the circle of love.

71 Love the animals of the wilderness and the deep waters and the fields, for when you give love even to those creatures who know you not, you gain a greater capacity to give and receive love from the people in your life that you do know. Such is the circle of love.

72 Love the plants and the mountains and the valleys and the forests and every life and place that is upon the earth, for as you love all that Elohim has made for you,

your heart opens to receive all the love that Elohim has for you. Such is the circle of love.

73 In loving all these, your kinsmen and all the world and everything therein, show gratitude to them and to Elohim, for with gratitude, you become worthy to receive all of the miracles Elohim would give to you.

74 Let it be known across the land that love is married to faith. Even in the face of great hardships and grief, do not abandon your faith in the reality and omnipotence of Elohim, for faith is the conduit to powers unseen and the channel through which all miracles flow, both the small and the great.

75 Therefore, waver not in the face of adversity, for only those who do not falter prove their faith is true and thus open the door to all the powers of Heaven.

76 Each day, choose to eat a variety of simple foods that retain life; various fruits and vegetables, sprouted bread, and sometimes a little honey for a treat. Such brings you both pleasure and health.

77 But if you were to eat only one food, such as dates, for every meal, and dates alone, you would soon become sickly and be very unhappy and disagreeable before that occurred from having to eat only dates for every meal.

78 Even as a wise man eats many different foods for happiness and health, so should you embrace balance in all of your thoughts and actions, if you desire to obtain happiness in life and true progression of your soul.

79 Too much of anything, even things which are wonderfully good, entombs a man in a grave he has dug, while moderation leads to a long life full of wonder and contentment.

80 If you nourish only one part of your life, you allow the other parts to recede, and all are needed for the journey.

81 It is fine to be a zealot for a short period of focus to gain a specific desire, but to be continually zealous to the point that reason and harmony hold no sway is to condemn yourself to contentions that trample lives that should instead be uplifted, both yours and those of whom you love.

82 But balance alone can be a false justification to squander the sands of your life, if you do not insure that virtue guides your path.

83 Elohim delights in the virtuous man and woman; virtue is the fruit of the tree of Celestine Light, and the sweetness thereof is made known to all, but tasted and savored only by the worthy.

84 Virtue is gentle and sleeps soundly at night. Virtue is faithful and kind. Virtue has patience and self-mastery. Virtue is peaceful and loving. Virtue is honest and reliable. Virtue is chaste and pure.

85 Find a virtuous man or woman, regardless of their religion or culture, and you will have found a true son or daughter of God.

86 To hold virtue in your life, you must instill it in your heart, so the habit to be virtuous becomes greater than the temptation to be unvirtuous.

87 By this, you conquer yourself; you defeat the adversary within; and in overcoming yourself, you become greater than he who conquers a city.

88 The capstone of the Temple of Forever is a golden sphere that has no beginning or end and

endless mysteries to discover hidden within. It is the admonition of Elohim that all who would walk the earth in righteousness would leave a legacy; that they might continue to uplift their brothers and sisters of spirit long after they have been freed from the bonds of mortality.

89 Even as Elohim has left you a legacy of the commandments of Sinai and the Eden of the earth and the true teachings of the prophets, that you might become more than you began.

90 As you see God do, so do you. You cannot give commandments unto men, nor can you reveal the truths of Heaven to the prophets, but as Elohim created the earth and everything therein, so you can create beauty and wonders which edify your brothers and sisters of spirit long after you have gone to your eternal reward.

91 As worthy, righteous, and virtuous Children of Light, true sons and daughters of God, let it be so."

BY THEIR FRUITS YOU SHALL KNOW THEM

Excerpted from the Oracles of Celestine Light: Vivus: Chapter 28

And it came to pass that Yeshua, Miriam, and his disciples departed from Ptolemais and walked a path to Bethsaida that traveled east over the ridge of hills.

2 They went out of their way to climb to the summit of a tall hill where they could look down upon Lake Gennesaret. At this place, they had their midday meal, and Philip asked a question to Yeshua that others had also wondered, saying, "Rabbi, we have just savored your words at Ptolemais, but I would ask you a question, not about what you said, but to whom you said it."

3 Yeshua rolled his hand, indicating that Philip should proceed, and Philip asked him, "In the synagogue, we have always been taught that we are the chosen people of God and that all other people are unworthy to have God's favor. Yet in Ptolemais, and also in Samaria, you have given your light and the wisdom of your words, and even mysteries and mighty miracles to those whom we have been told since our youth should be scorned.

4 In Ptolemais, I think there were more Romans, Greeks, Syrians, and other foreigners than there were

Hebrews hearing your words. I must confess that I am confused." And all of the disciples nodded their heads in agreement.

5 Yeshua answered them, saying, "I am thankful you have asked me this and were not afraid. And I hope it will always be so, for it is important that you understand the fullness of the Celestine Light.

6 But I have spoken about this already to you; how is it that you have not understood the words I have said?

7 If my own disciples cannot comprehend this most basic truth, how will others see the light?

8 Every person on this world is a spirit son and daughter of our Father and Mother in Heaven, who loved their children and helped them to grow before they were born upon the earth.

9 Therefore, every man and woman is truly a brother and sister of one another.

10 Each is a child of God, so how could it be that Elohim would look upon all of the souls upon the earth and say this small number here alone will we love. Only these few will we bless or acknowledge or give an inheritance in our Kingdom.

11 The ignorant and the prejudice look for ways to puff themselves up by tearing others down. They will say, 'These people are not of our tribes, and they do not live the laws of God. Therefore, their inheritance is desolation and separation.'

12 But I have said unto you that I have come to destroy the laws that mock the true Celestine Light of Elohim, for man has elevated falsehoods to sacredness for his own purposes.

13 I bring the fullness of the Celestine fire, which most will not be able to bear, but that you, my brothers, must not falter in, even though because of it, those whom it scorches will try to bring death and torment to some of you in retaliation.

14 I came first to the Hebrews because in important times past, their fathers were faithful to the simple commandments of Elohim.

15 Elohim the Father made a solemn promise to the faithful Hebrews of ancient days that the fullness of the Celestine Light would be brought first to their descendants.

16 I am the fulfillment of that promise, and when I first spoke of the light, it was to the Hebrews, in the cities and towns of the Hebrews.

17 But I am not the light to the Hebrews alone, but the embodiment of the Celestine Light of Elohim to all the world, and everyone is my brother and sister of spirit.

18 There are some parts of the Celestine Light which the Hebrews know and do well; to them, I teach the parts that they do not know or do well.

19 So too there are parts of the Celestine Light which many Gentiles know and do well; to them, I will also teach the parts they do not know or do well whenever the opportunity comes upon me to share the Celestine Light with them.

20 If man is to become more than he is, if war is to cease and peace is to reign, then man must have respect for others beyond his tribe, beyond his nation, and beyond his practices and traditions and beliefs in God.

21 It is a foolish man of any religion who thinks that

Elohim has given hundreds of laws that man must follow to please God.

22 Elohim gives no commandments to the children of men save the Great Commandment and the Twelve Commandments of Sinai, and these not to burden man but to uplift him and help him to become more than he began.

23 All other laws, be they written in the scriptures or not, are given by men to control other men.

24 Now the spirit of the Great Commandment and the commandments of Sinai do not need to be written upon scrolls of scripture to be known, for these principles are a yearning of the soul. They are inscribed upon the heart of every man and woman before they are born into a physical life by Elohim the Mother.

25 Through the teachings of parents and priests and cultures and traditions and actions that are contrary, the fullness of the true commandments may become lost in the hearts and heads of some men and women, and the light all but extinguished because of these things.

26 Yet even when a man commits acts contrary to the Great Commandment and the commandments of Sinai, there will continue to be a still, small voice whispering to him in his head and a feeling in his heart that what he does is contrary to the will of God and contrary to his own happiness and well-being.

27 Only after he has repeated the same error many times will he become deaf to the still, small voice and the flutter in his heart, and hear and feel it no more.

28 Yet even then, in a place inside he keeps imprisoned and never visits, the Celestine Light will whisper

reminding him that he does wrong. And sometimes despite all his best efforts to convince himself otherwise, the truth he has hidden from himself will come to torment his consciousness.

29 Now I ask you: Who are the chosen people of God? I tell you plainly. They are not of any one tribe, or any one people, or any one nation, or any one religion.

30 Verily, the chosen people of God are they who keep the spirit of the Great Commandment and the commandments of Sinai and by this live the essence of the Celestine Light. And the tribe they are from, or the people they are a part of, or the nation they live in, or the religion they believe in, are all nothing of consequence in the eyes of the Elohim.

31 And what is the spirit? What is the essence? Love God, be respectful and a good neighbor to all people, be virtuous and of good character in your words and deeds, be of service to others, and be a good steward over all that you have been given responsibility over, beginning with the temple of your body.

32 How then may you know a Child of Light? You will know them by the fruits of their life. How well do they live the spirit of the few true commandments of God and the essence of the Celestine Light?

33 It does not matter whether they are Hebrew, Roman, Greek, Syrian, or someone from any other tribe or land. If they live the spirit of the true commandments, they are sons and daughters of God, true to the Celestine Light within them.

34 Seek them out and do not turn them away because they are not exactly like you, for these are your true

brothers and sisters of the light."

35 As Yeshua took a pause in speaking, Yohhanan asked, "Rabbi, what you say resonates in my heart, but I am still having difficulties in my head. You say that if men hold to the spirit of the true commandments and the essence of the Celestine Light, they will be numbered among the chosen, even if they are Greeks or Romans or other people.

36 But the commandments are very specific, even as the second commandment of Sinai says to only worship Elohim and even condemns veneration of anything except Elohim.

37 I have seen the ways of the Greeks and Romans and some of other people. They do not even know the name of Elohim. Some of them may be virtuous and of good character and good stewards, but they worship a myriad of false gods and venerate many objects and places. How then can they be numbered among the chosen?"

38 And Yeshua answered him, saying, "Men are not held accountable for that which they know not, but only for that which they know. The essence of the Celestine Light and the virtues of the Great Commandment and the commandments of Sinai are etched into the soul of every man and woman born upon the earth. But the beliefs of religion, including the name and substance of God, are taught differently within the family and the tribe.

39 Concerning the nature of God, as the children are taught, so they believe until they are shown the true light. Then the true light kindles a fire in their heart that

they did not even know was there.

40 If a man from another land has been taught that God is a big rock that sticks up from the ground and he leads his life in righteousness, with virtue and good character, worshiping the big rock in the faithfulness of his beliefs, he has as much favor with Elohim as the man who knows and faithfully follows the Elohim.

41 It is the virtues and good character that distinguish a Child of Light, and they are not held accountable for the realities of the nature and fullness of God until they have had the opportunity to be taught and understand them fully.

42 It is for this purpose that you have been called to be my disciples. You learn from me now, but the day soon comes when I shall send you out into the world to preach the Gospel I have taught you and bring a portion of the Celestine Light I have given you to those who will rejoice when you come.

43 Many will hate and revile you because of me, but some will open their hearts to you and receive the Celestine Light, which will be much greater and fulfilling than the light they had previously held in their beliefs.

44 The principles of virtue and character that I teach, which is the spirit of the true commandments and the essence of the Celestine Light, will spread forth across the world through you and those who come after you, for the Children of Light wait with a yearning heart for what they know not, until it is upon them, and then great will be their joy.

45 Millennia will pass, and many men will become

more wicked than their forefathers; but because of the seeds you plant, some men will become more righteous, preparing the way for the fullness of the Celestine Light of Elohim upon the world and the beginning of the Epoch of Promise.

46 Therefore, when you are sent out into the world to bring souls to the light, remember to find the Children of Light who are waiting for you, not by their tribe or nation or beliefs, but by their fruits.

47 By their fruits, you shall know them."

THE NATURE OF ETERNITY

(Yeshua's Sermon at the funeral of
Yochanan the Baptizer)

Excerpted from the Oracles of Celestine Light: Vivus: Chapter 30

And it came to pass on the following day that the body of Yochanan was wrapped in a simple knotted, white linen shroud and buried in a tomb owned by Martha's father in a hillside northwest of Bethany.

16 Over one thousand people followed the funeral procession and watched in silence as Yochanan's body was interred and the tomb was sealed.

17 Then the father of Martha spoke to the people assembled at the foot of the tomb, saying that Yochanan was a good man who walked with God. And he thanked them for coming to give him their respect.

18 As he sat down, he asked Yeshua to speak also to the people. And Yeshua rose up, and standing in front of the tomb, he said unto them, "It is good to grieve, to cry, and to acknowledge the empty place in your life when one you love is no longer there to hold you and make you laugh and comfort you just by their physical presence.

19 But in your grief, know this with certainty: As surely as the sun rises in the sky, so too rise the souls

of all who have died to their reward in an eternity that never ends.

20 Those you love wait for you still, and the virtuous need not fear separation, for mortality is but a heartbeat, and in eternity, they shall not be parted.

21 As in Adam, save for a precious few, all will die a physical death. The spirit essence will rise to the realms Elohim created for eternity. And because of the love of Elohim, everyone shall live again in the spirit.

22 But unto the virtuous and righteous, it is given not only to live again in the spirit, but for your immortal soul to become one with a glorified new physical body, made whole and perfect by Elohim, for your life eternal.

23 Your future began with your past, for your existence is an eternal walk that never ends.

24 Before you were born of woman, your spirit was created by Elohim, and before it was born upon the earth, the spirit of all things lived in a spiritual realm called Koropean.

25 And to the Koropean, the realm of spirit, all things of spirit born into a physical existence shall someday return, even the birds in the air, the fish in the sea, and every blade of grass beneath your feet.

26 So vast it is in expanse that the earthly mind of man cannot even begin to comprehend the magnitude and diversity of the Koropean.

27 Verily, there is nothing that lives or that has lived or that will ever live upon the earth whose spirit was not first created by the Elohim and then existed in the Koropean. Nor is there anything or anyone that has ever lived that shall not return to that realm.

28 But everything that has a spirit does not also have a soul, for only the children of men and women, whose spirits were all birthed in a sacred union of love by your Father and Mother in Heaven, have been given a soul; and more precious than all the treasure of earth, it is.
29 For a soul created in the celestial union of love, it is given an ember of divinity that ever calls the soul to a greater light called Celestine, that it might ever be moved to return to the blessed Kingdom from which it came, expanded in stature from its humble beginnings.
30 When the soul comes to earth and it is born of woman into a body of flesh and bones, it dwells in the body of a man or a woman and is thrust into a physical world of darkness and light.
31 Mortality is the crucible, the refiner's fire, and the soul within the body ever beckons to the light, even while the physical man or woman in the body is ever seduced to darkness by the temptations of the world and the pleasures of the body.
32 Therefore, man has been given the years of his life to feel the warmth of his soul calling him out of darkness and back to the Celestine Light that is his home.
33 Throughout the days of his mortal life, the warmth of the ember of divinity ever burns quietly within the heart of man: that he may always know good from evil and right from wrong; that on the day of the Judgment of Resonance, he may be weighed in the balance by his own choices and not be able to say, 'I did not know.'
34 Therefore, take heed, for you know not which breath upon the earth shall be your last, whether your life will end when you are young or when you are old.

35 I say unto you, do not ignore the warm and gentle calling of the divine ember of light burning in your bosom. It is calling you from your mundane life to the glory that you can be.

36 Think not to say, 'Today I will eat, drink and be merry, for I still have my old age to become virtuous,' for though you may be young, these may be the last days of your old age.

37 When your physical body is laid in the grave, your soul held within your spirit rises immediately to the first Judgment of Resonance, at the place of transition in the Koropean realm.

38 For a moment, whatever you believed the afterlife to be will seem to be as it is, but then at the direction of Elohim, the angels of Heaven will come and the illusion will vanish like a mirage on the desert, and the reality of eternity will become apparent.

39 The angels of Elohim shall look with you at the life you have lived in mortality and the virtue you had or had not.

40 Every iota shall not be reviewed; not the rivulets, only the rivers.

41 Then you shall be inexorably drawn to the place of your resonance within the Koropean: the virtuous to a place of warmth and light and the unvirtuous to a place of bitter cold and darkness; the greater the virtue, the brighter the light; the less the virtue, the deeper the darkness.

42 It matters not whether you are of Judah or Samaria or Rome, whether you are a man or a woman, whether you were rich or poor, whether you lived free or as a

slave.

43 Each shall be judged, not by what they believed or who they were, but by what they did and even by what they thought but did not do.

44 Did you live a life of virtue? Did you uphold the Great Commandment and the commandments of Sinai as the ember of God within you ever beckoned and guided you to do?

45 Your spirit shall again have a form of a physical man or woman without the substance, and your soul will dwell within it.

46 Those in the Celestine Light will be among their friends and family who also had virtue, and they shall have joy together and delight in new knowledge and opportunities.

47 Those that are in darkness shall be among others in the darkness, but none that they know or love or miss or take pleasure to be around.

48 Misery and loneliness shall be the lot of those in the darkness. Their only hope will not be for new knowledge and opportunity like those in the light, but simply to regain that which was lost by their foolishness.

49 Though beset by the pain of their own mistakes, those in the darkness will still have a promise. From the lonely place of cold and dreariness where they dwell in misery, far and away, they will see a distant lamp shining from the realm of warmth and happiness, illuminating the path they can still walk to come back into the light, with faith and repentance, and sorrow and confession and restitution and good works.

50 For each moment, whether one is in the darkness

or in the light, every spirit will continue to make choices that can show virtue or vice. As they act upon their choices, they will move either into a greater light or into a deeper darkness.

51 Then at an hour you know not, nor expect, will come a final Judgment of Resonance upon your soul.

52 Verily, all men and women who have ever lived shall stand someday before the Elohim to be weighed in the balance and judged, not only of their life in mortality, but also their life before mortality and after it.

53 And all the angels of Heaven shall stand as witnesses on the day of your final judgment.

54 So shall every person whose life was ever touched for good or evil, by those being weighed, also stand as witnesses to see the life before them, with nothing hidden.

55 Nor shall anything that was done, not be seen, for at the final judgment, every iota shall be judged. Of your thoughts and of your actions, both good and bad, from your entire mortal life, nothing shall be hidden.

56 With every good and virtuous deed you ever thought or did, light will flow to and be added to the essence of your soul.

57 And with every evil or loathsome thing you ever thought or did, light will flow out of and be taken away from the essence of your soul.

58 When all has been seen, your soul will be weighed in the balance, and those who lived selfishly, without virtue and kindness and gratitude and stewardship, shall be found wanting.

59 The virtuous will be pulled by resonance of their

own light into warmth and greater light, and they shall be given a new and perfected, immortal physical body and live near the presence of Elohim in the Celestine Realm. They shall be given great blessings and new stewardships worthy of their light.

60 But those lacking virtue shall be pulled by their own dark resonance into a bitter cold and deeper darkness, where there shall be weeping and wailing and gnashing of teeth and an endless torment upon the soul for the warmth and light that could have been.

61 But remember, even this is not the end, but only the beginning. The love and forgiveness of the Father and Mother is boundless, and even those in outer darkness can still reach the Celestine Light and savor the warmth and the love of paradise among their family and friends and gain new knowledge and be given a greater stewardship.

62 Even in outer darkness, they will have the choice to do good or do evil, and when the good weighs more than the evil, they will draw light to their soul.

63 After millennia, if they continue to seek the light and do good, their balance shall be with the light, and they will inherit the just reward they deserve after overcoming the suffering and punishments they inflicted upon themselves.

64 Knowing this—that for lack of virtue in mortality your soul could be in torment for millennia—may each of you choose the light each day.

65 There is still another path in the afterlife, one bestowed upon few, and that is to return again to mortality. This was the path that had been given to

Yochanan by Elohim.

66 For Yochanan is a choice soul who has faithfully served Elohim from before the creation of the world. Your ancestors knew him as Elijah the Prophet, and so great was his vision and power to sway the hearts of men that after he had died in the flesh and had risen to his glory, he was asked by Elohim to come again into the flesh, that the world might hear his voice once more; that he might prepare the world for the greater light to come.

67 Thus was the scripture fulfilled saying, 'Behold, I send my messenger before thy face, who shall prepare the way before you.'

68 Therefore, when you remember Yochanan, his laugh, his honesty and frankness, his simple words of power, and his example of a life of virtue and righteousness, remember that you had a true prophet of the most high walking among you.

69 You had a man who had been born twice of woman, walking among you.

70 My hope for each of you is that you will remember this glorious son of God and live your life as he showed us how to live: full of spirit and love and unwavering virtue and faith.

71 And for those of his family, know that he waits for you even now and that mortality is but a heartbeat of eternity. I admonish you to live in virtue, doing good upon the earth, fulfilling your stewardships, and surely, you will be together again and for all eternity to come."

72 Then Yeshua slapped his hands together and proclaimed, "Now, let us rejoice! Play glad music,

prepare a feast, talk with one another, and remember Yochanan. Celebrate and thank this wonderful man of God who served you all of his days!"

SERMON IN CAPHARSALAMA

Excerpted from the Oracles of Celestine Light: Vivus: Chapter 33

And it came to pass that Yeshua and the disciples mingled and spoke with the men from Capharsalama for some time, standing on the road outside of town. They introduced themselves and told of their families and their experiences with Yeshua.

18 Gimiel asked Yeshua, "Would you bless us with a sermon while you are here? For we may never again have you among us."

19 "Of course, Gimiel," Yeshua answered. "Let us pass through the town and you can gather those who would desire to hear my words. On the small hill north of town, I will speak at the midday."

20 And it came to pass that upon the midday, Yeshua and his disciples sat atop the small hill and a crowd of over two hundred men, women, and children came to hear him speak. The men sat to one side and the women and children to another, as was the way of the people of Capharsalama.

21 Some had brought food with them to eat their midday meal while listening to his words, but most had not, and seeing this, Yeshua asked that those who had brought food would bring it to his disciples so that they

might share it and distribute it to all.

22 Those with food came up to the hill and gave the disciples the fish, bread, vegetables, and cheese that they had brought, and it filled four small baskets.

23 Looking at the small amount of food and the large number of people, Yohhanan commented to no one in particular, "There will only be enough for each person to have maybe one or two bites."

24 Then Yeshua came and blessed the food, saying, "Our Father and Mother in Heaven, we are grateful for this bounty and the good earth, which has borne it. We ask your blessings upon it, that it will come forth in abundance and deliciousness, that all might be filled and nourished."

25 He beckoned for the disciples to bring some large empty baskets, and taking a loaf of bread from one of the small baskets, he began to break it into large chunks and place them inside the larger basket. Soon the larger basket was filled, and he bade some of the men from Capharsalama to distribute it to the people.

26 Likewise, using two hands, he scooped several of the small fish from the smaller basket and placed them into the larger basket and continued to do this until the larger basket was filled to a weight that two men could carry and then bade some men from Capharsalama to make sure each person had enough for their satisfaction and to return for more if they were lacking.

27 In like manner were the vegetables and cheese distributed. And the disciples were astounded by the miracle they were witnessing as the four small baskets never diminished the food they held, even though the

items from them filled several larger baskets.

28 Even among the people of Capharsalama, it became evident that there was far more food remaining after they had all eaten their fill than had been present before the first bite had been taken. And seeing this, they spoke in quiet wonder to one another and gave great attention to Yeshua as he began to speak.

29 And Yeshua said unto them, "My brothers and sisters of Capharsalama, when I was last here, I heard much about the law and what the law as recorded in the scrolls of the prophets say about the things you can and cannot do in your life. These laws are said to be from Elohim; therefore, who cannot obey them without condemnation? The penalty for disobedience, for even small things, is severe. And for greater things, death awaits.

30 Knowing a sword hangs ever over your head lest you take too many steps on the Sabbath or eat or touch something that is unclean, or (pointing to the crowd) sit men with women, does the fear of the law and the punishments therein not weigh upon you and cause you to act or not act from fear, rather than love of God?

31 I speak now as I spoke before when I came upon your town. Because I see you are very devout in keeping the law, I will speak more upon it because of my love for you.

32 Only man can craft a god that must be obeyed because of fear not love. Only man can create a god who demands actions which are contrary to common sense and God's own interest.

33 Every person upon the earth lives today because

Elohim made alive their first ancestors in the Garden of Eden. Just as your children are a part of you, so every person who has ever walked the earth from the descendants of the garden has a spark of God within them.

34 Every man from every country is your brother, and every woman from every country is your sister.

35 I say unto you with words of soberness that every man and woman upon the earth is a child of God.

36 Would you kill your own children because they disobeyed you in some slight thing or even in some great thing? How about your neighbor's children? How about the children of the Egyptians or the Romans?

37 I hope you would not. Do you think that Elohim, a God that is real and living, and not a contrived creation of men, would demand some of the children upon the earth to kill others or would give favor to some over others, when all are children of Elohim?

38 Would a God that created all people as equal sons and daughters demand that some be sacrificed at the altar, slaughtered in war, or given as plunder to be raped and enslaved?

39 Could you separate your children and say, 'These will find my favor, but these are to be raped, enslaved, and killed as needs be?"

40 Do you truly believe that a true and living God, creator of all that is, father and mother of all the children of men, would ever treat their children so blessed with love in creation to such a despicable and ignominious end?

41 You have heard it said that it is easier for Heaven

and earth to pass away than for the smallest of the laws to pass away. But I say unto you it is easier for a lamb to get into Heaven than for a man who obeys a law that is contrary to the very essence of Elohim.

42 Elohim is love.

43 Elohim is inspiration.

44 Elohim is fair and just.

45 Elohim is compassionate and understanding.

46 Elohim loves virtue in whomever it is found and gives no preference to one child over another for any other reason.

47 Elohim cherishes the life of all things that have been created and blesses the man that honors and protects life.

48 But men who take life without necessity for food or in self-defense bring a curse upon themselves, not from Elohim, but from their own soul, for their inner guilt cries out for the sin they have done against God.

49 Consider how you would be if you were the perfect father or the perfect mother to your children; as you would so be, even so is Elohim many times more to each of you, the children of God.

50 Nor would true laws of the true God demand the beauty of the body to be hidden. What would be the point to create the most magnificent work of art that is, the human body, only to hide it forever under great coverings of clothing?

51 If the body is not hidden but seen, there is greater incentive to honor it and honor the creator by keeping it fit and trim. But if it is forever hidden under flowing and voluminous clothing, with only the eyes and the feet to

be seen, then it can be allowed to get fat and sagging, for who will know or see it to condemn the poor steward?

52 And why do you think men and women lust for one another? Is it evil as many would have you believe? Consider that it is a desire Elohim instilled in every person. How then can a gift of God be evil?

53 Is it simply to insure the race of men perpetuates as others proclaim? If that were so, then you would cease to have desires of that kind once you were beyond the age of fertility, for there would be no need for such desires. But any of you who have passed that age know of a certainty that the desire remains.

54 Verily, I declare unto you that you desire one another and can give physical pleasure to one another because that is a gift from Elohim that you might always have a source of joy and pleasure, even if you do not have a single coin or a roof over your head or food to eat; and not just any joy or pleasure, but one that fills you with a glow that lasts and a happiness that does not diminish with the waning day.

55 But in this joy, procreation does bear weight, for within the true laws of Elohim, the Great Commandment says to multiply and fill the earth and the commandments of Sinai say to not fornicate or commit adultery.

56 Therefore, it is only in righteousness that men and women may quench the fires of their lust, only within the halo of a marriage, given before witnesses, with commitment for life.

57 Elohim gave the commandments; Elohim gave the desire that stirs the loins; and these two were given that

they might be fulfilled in each other, even as the man and woman are fulfilled in one another.

58 Marriage then becomes the only resolution that honors God and fulfills the desires that stir the loins.

59 It is for children that all of this is so, that they might be born into homes of balance and light and have the best chance to grow into balance and light in their lives.

60 And it is for the parents that they might overcome their weaknesses and selfishness and make their weaknesses their strengths.

61 But never forget this total pleasure has been given to you by Elohim to enjoy, and enjoy often for all of your life.

62 Remember, the time to procreate is but a few hours in your lives; all the other days Elohim has given this great gift of pleasure and comfort and love, that you might have joy and fulfillment that is above the cares of the world."

63 Bending his left arm and holding his chin with his hand, Yeshua looked toward the heavens and asked aloud, "Let us consider what other laws of the prophets can be revealed as merely the foolishness of men who would be kings over their brethren.

64 Certainly, circumcision must fall into this pit. Consider that if circumcision was necessary or important, the sons of men would be born from the womb already circumcised.

65 Who is man to cut up a child made in the image of God so that the child is no longer in the image of God? Why would Elohim create a child one way only to ask the child to be disfigured by men once he was born?

66 They say it is to distinguish the sons of Israel from the Gentiles and to show obedience to God, but I say unto you if that were important, the sons of Israel would have been born circumcised.

67 Verily, Elohim would ask men to cut off their own finger to show obedience before they would ask them to cut an innocent and defenseless child.

68 In my condemnation of the law, know that I do not condemn all of it for there are some parts that are reasonable and just, but they are few and the unreasonable and unjust are many.

69 Therefore, I will teach you some of the signs by which you can judge a law of Elohim from a law of men in the scrolls of the prophets.

70 If obedience to a law gives Celestine Light to your life and only light and causes the light within you to shine and to always shine, then it is of Elohim and you should give it a place in your heart and life.

71 Respect those laws which have eternal significance and bring Celestine Light to you. Cherish those laws and live them as your life.

72 Do not listen to the interpretations of men, concerning the law and the prophets, for many are the laws of man that have been said to be the laws of God but have no value in the world to come or value in the world in which you now live.

73 Verily, if it is of God, it will have eternal significance and will bring Celestine Light into your life, and if it is of man, it will have no consideration or merit for your entry into glory in Heaven and, instead, will often be onerous and not of light.

74 The ways of Elohim are simple to live and easy to understand, not convoluted and ritualistic like the ways of men and the religions of men.

75 The laws of men have no meaning in the world to come, but the laws of Elohim involve the purity of your heart and your good works in this life, and those jewels of character have great weight on the day of eternal judgment.

76 If a law is of man, it will give power to men to judge the spiritual correctness of other men, and God has not given to men to judge the spiritual worth of souls or to take life or abase the spirit of the children of God upon the earth.

77 Nevertheless, there are some things in the traditions and the law of the prophets that are true and worthy, given for your benefit and edification; and these are easy to recognize, for they have significance both in this world and the world to come.

78 Verily, if that which is given or expected expands your spirit, or is for your health or for the strength of your family, or for building your good character, or for helping your relationships to be deeper and more fulfilling, or to increase your knowledge, and does not demean you or take away your spirit or constrain your finite time upon the earth or hurt others and keeps balance in your life and promotes harmony and peace in your heart and among all men and women, then you may know that it is good and of God."

79 Then Yeshua stopped speaking, and gathering his wife and his disciples, he bade the people of Capharsalama farewell, for he desired still to travel far

upon this day.

SERMON ON THE MOUNT

PART 1

Excerpted from the Oracles of Celestine Light: Vivus: Chapter 45

The following day, at sunrise, Salome first learned the Contemplative Movements as she stood barefoot upon the ground outside of the house of Yeshua, following the movements she watched Yeshua, Miriam, Martha, and the children doing and listening as Yeshua explained the significance of each movement while he was doing them.

2 Miriam gave her some of her garments to wear, and they put away Salome's expensive bejeweled clothes from the palace so that undue attention would not be drawn to her.

3 Later, Yeshua told the Apostles who she was, but asked them not to reveal her true identity to others for a time.

4 From that day forth, she remained with Yeshua, Miriam, and Martha, and if there were any who condemned them, it was only in their thoughts, for none spoke ill of the arrangement.

5 Within a week, a small room had been added to Yeshua's house by three men from the community so Salome could have a place of privacy of her own as he had promised.

6 Soon after daybreak, multitudes of people began to gather at Yeshua's house from every direction.

7 The eleven Apostles came with their families within two hours of first light, as Yeshua had asked them to do the previous day.

8 Some people called out from the crowd for Yeshua to heal them or to heal one of their relatives that were with them, but he moved about as if he had not heard them.

9 Once Cephas arrived, he spoke to the multitude and asked them to have patience and promised that Yeshua would speak to them soon. And they were calmed by his words insomuch that no longer did any call out to Yeshua to be healed.

10 On the third hour of light, Yeshua, Miriam, and the Apostles commenced a walk toward the hills to the west and all of the people, including Salome and Martha and the children, followed them.

11 The day was beautiful, warm, and sunny, and there was almost a festive atmosphere as people spoke with smiles and cordiality as they followed Yeshua up into the hills.

12 Northwest of Chorazin, about the distance to Capernaum, was a large hillock, and upon this hill, Yeshua and the Apostles settled at the top and the multitude sat down on the ground below him, spreading their linens and setting up their sun tarps. Many of the children played at the base of the hill while their parents sat up higher to hear the words of Yeshua.

13 Spreading and raising both hands high into the air, Yeshua said unto them, "On this beautiful day, with the

sun's light and warmth upon you, and the blue sky above you, and the green hills beyond, and the magnificent expanse of lake below, and the songs of birds upon the air, give thanks to Elohim for the glorious world that was made for you to live upon.

14 And I say unto you: Blessed are those who are humble in spirit, for humility opens the gate of Heaven.

15 Blessed are the challenged; those who long to live in the Celestine Light, but are faced with many impediments which block the path to the light. Elohim shall give them comfort.

16 Blessed are the calm; those who are not overcome by their own desires or the chaos around them, but trust in God. They shall have peace in their hearts in the world and inherit the earth to come.

17 Blessed are they who hunger and thirst after righteousness. They hearken to the still, small voice and, with desire and action, seek to fulfill the will of God. They shall be filled overflowing with the Celestine Light that they seek.

18 Blessed are the merciful, who see in the misfortune of others their own life that could be and help others as they would wish to be helped, not just with alms, but also by giving of themselves and their time. They shall be blessed with the mercy of the Almighty.

19 Blessed are the pure in heart; those who are upright and sincere, honest in every thought and activity. They will have the Holy Spirit abiding always with them, and they shall see God with a special witness.

20 Blessed are the peacemakers, both among nations and among neighbors, those who have a peaceful mind

and a harmonious heart to resolve the disputes of men. They shall be the treasurers of Elohim, guiding divine peace from the heavens to light the lives of men upon the earth. And they shall be called the Children of God.

21 Blessed are those who are persecuted for righteousness sake; they that live the highest light despite the condemnation of the world. They shall rise a step in Heaven for every lash they take upon the world, and the Kingdom of Heaven shall be theirs.

22 Blessed are you, when you resist evil, and men revile you and persecute you by word and deed and say all manner of evil against you falsely, for my sake.

23 Rejoice and be exceedingly glad, for great is your reward in Heaven, and thus did they persecute the prophets which were before you.

24 You are the salt of the earth, but take heed not to lose your savor or be contaminated by the impure; else with what will the food find its flavor? It would thenceforth be good for nothing, but to be cast out and trodden under the feet of men.

25 You are the Celestine Light of the world. In the example of your life, how you eat and speak and dress and live, you should be as a city upon a hill that cannot be hidden.

26 For you do not light a candle and then hide it under a basket, but put it on a tall candlestick that it can give light to all who are in the house.

27 The world is your house. Therefore, do not hide the Celestine Light of Elohim that burns within you, but hold it high that all the world might be illuminated by your light.

28 Let your light so shine before the world that those who condemn you will know in their hearts that they condemn a Child of God and that those who are lost Children of Elohim will see your light and find their way home.

29 Think not that I have come to uphold the law and the prophets, for I have not come to uphold any but those of truth and to fulfill the promise of Elohim given to men and destroy those that are not.

30 And there is far more to be trampled underfoot than to be upheld, for the teachings of God have been taken and the teachings of man have been given.

31 I am he who is the builder, and I have come to tear down the feeble works of man and to restore the mighty temple of God.

32 Some of you here are of the world, but conquer yourself and you can be numbered among the Children of Light.

33 Some of you here are Children of Light that have been lost in the world, and now you have found the source of the light, but cannot see how to reconcile the life you have lived with the life you know you should live.

34 Choose that which has eternal significance and you shall have joy, both in this life and the life to come.

35 Some of you here are Children of Light who have committed in your heart and shown by your deeds that you are Children of Light indeed.

36 Unto you, I say that your righteousness must exceed the righteousness of the scribes and Pharisees, for much has been given to you and much is expected.

37 You know that it is the law that you shall not murder, and whosoever murders another shall be judged in both this life and the next.

38 But I say unto you that there are far more ways to murder than killing the body, and all are accountable to God and should be accountable to the laws of men.

39 Therefore, let whoever has a raging anger against another, be it a man or a woman or an animal, be liable to judgment on the earth, even as they shall be in Heaven.

40 For a raging anger is a murderous anger. It is an anger that misses the final blow of murder only because of fear of the consequences.

41 Therefore, I say unto you that a man who has barely controlled anger without a righteous cause and injures a man or a woman or an animal, either in their body or their spirit, must be judged the same as the man who attempted murder and failed.

42 Knowing this, let peace and calm always flow in the heart and mind and thoughts and words of the Children of Light, save in defense against that which is unrighteous.

43 When you speak, speak with respect to all men, and to all women, and to all who work for you, and to all animals. Though you may command them to do this or to do that, do it only with kindness in your words and respect in your thoughts and actions, except for those who do not reciprocate the respect which you give.

44 And if a Child of Light should curse another person without cause or spit Raca unto another, giving contempt without cause, let him come before the

council and be held accountable for his actions.

45 Let the Children of Light always be the embodiment of the Celestine Light, especially among one another, especially among husbands and wives and their children.

46 If you have a disagreement with someone, speak of it together and come to a solution with words and reason and respect and love.

47 Do not sulk in silence, for that is only fuel for the fire and shows a disrespect, not just for others, but for yourself and for Elohim.

48 Almost as bad as anger is to treat another, especially a husband, wife, or child, as if they are an idiot and that their thoughts and opinions are not even of worth to listen to with intent to hear.

49 To not listen with respect to the thoughts and opinions of your husband, wife, or children, or brothers and sisters of light, even when you are in disagreement or even when they are simple in their method of explanation, is a grievous sin in the eyes of Elohim, needing not only repentance before God, but restitution to those you have wronged by your words and actions.

50 When you are wrong, admit your wrong with humility and ask the forgiveness of both God and the person you have wronged. And prove your sincerity by restitution to the person you have wronged.

51 Do not think you can alleviate your sin by making an offering before the altar of God and then go your way. First, you must be reconciled with whoever you have wronged, and only then will Elohim recognize your gift before the altar.

52 Do not be hardheaded and unreasonable when

you are in the hands of your adversaries, nor docile like a sheep, allowing others to do with you as they will. Endeavor to give them no cause to do worse to you while you are in their hands, but neither stand idle in defense of righteousness and fairness.

53 Keep your peace until you can stand before the fair and impartial to present the facts. If no fair and impartial are to be found, call upon Elohim to deliver you.

54 You know that by the laws of God and men, it is said that you shall not commit adultery.

55 But I say unto you that whosoever looks upon a married woman or man with lust in their thoughts has already committed adultery in their heart.

56 You see my wife Miriam, beautiful, with her face uncovered, and it is not a sin to look upon her. Nor is it a sin to look upon her and admire her beauty, for she is a creation of Elohim, and you honor Elohim by admiring the creations of Elohim. It would be no different if she were standing here before you naked in all of her splendor.

57 Yet the man who looks upon her with lust, who thinks impure thoughts of her, but does not act upon his thoughts by either word or deed for fear of the consequences, has nevertheless already committed adultery in his heart.

58 This silent adultery may not be punished by man, for it is kept hidden and unknown from men. But it is known to Elohim and shall be punished by God, both in this life and the next.

59 Therefore, if you are weak to lust, you must separate

yourself from the temptation, lest you are burned by the fire you start.

60 If your eyes cause you to sin, cover your eyes that you will not see the temptation, for it is better that you are blind to temptation than your whole body and soul is cast into the rubbish dump.

61 Verily, your eyes are the windows of your soul, and what your eyes see, your body becomes. Therefore, let your eyes be focused only upon righteousness, that your whole life may be full of light.

62 And if your right hand is causing you to sin, tie it to your side, lest it lead your whole body away from the light; so demeaned of value that it must be cast into the garbage pile of Ge Hinnom and burned in the fire.

63 Now lust is the greatest temptation of the adversary within: lust for a woman or man, lust for power, lust of gluttony, lust for money. All things of lust lead man to commit acts for which the eternal consequences are far more painful and enduring than the pleasure of the fleeting fulfillment, which is here today and gone tomorrow.

64 Of these, lust for a woman, be she married or not, often clouds the better judgment of man, more so than all other types of lust. Therefore, against this lust must you ever guard.

65 To prevent this lust, by law and tradition, women cover themselves from head to toe in uncomfortable garments that men cannot look upon them and lust.

66 Yet it is not the woman who is sinning, but the man. Therefore, it should not be the woman who must be covered in uncomfortable coverings, but the man.

67 Let the woman dress in comfort and freedom. And if a man finds that seeing the bare skin of a woman causes him to lust, then let the man hide himself away in his house or cover his eyes with a hood or coverings so that he is nearly blind. The woman should not have to suffer because of the sin of the man.

68 That the fires of lust may be righteously quenched, all men and women should also be wed, and this they should do while they are young, shortly after their eighteenth celebration of birth, that the natural lust which Elohim gave to men and women for pleasure and procreation can be satisfied righteously within the bonds of marriage.

69 For the man or woman who is receiving pleasure and fulfillment within their marriage will not give into temptation to look elsewhere.

70 It has always been so, since the beginning of time, that there are more righteous women of light than there are men of light.

71 This will not be changed by all the proselytizing and preaching that you may do, for Elohim has always sent down into the bodies of women, the greater portion of the virtuous and faithful spirits of Heaven.

72 Therefore, let some among the righteous men of the Children of Light take another wife, one chosen with love by the wife they have, that all righteous women will have the opportunity to be married to virtuous men in this life.

73 And a plural marriage is not just a man to another woman, but also the new wife to the wife that stands already with the man, and among them there shall be

no secrets.

74 Nor is it meant for women to be always with child, for how then are they to have a life beyond caring for children? And this is easier to accomplish in righteousness in a house with multiple wives.

75 Verily, the spirits of Heaven wait with joy to come down into a body upon the earth, that they might further grow and expand their light by their choices and experiences.

76 But use alternatives in your intimacy to insure you do not bring children into the world until you are prepared to nurture their hearts, bodies, minds, and spirits, for all who are married will be held accountable, not only for choosing in selfishness to not have children, but also for choosing to have children when they were not prepared to care for them in all ways to encourage their growth, expansion, and happiness.

77 It has been the law that whosoever desires to put away his wife shall give her a certificate of divorce.

78 But I say unto you that wives may put away their husbands as well for just cause and demand lifelong support.

79 But neither the husband nor the wife shall put away the other, save it be for just cause, which is fornication or adultery, or violent or continual torment of the spirit, mind, or body.

80 And whosoever marries someone who has been divorced for fornication or adultery commits adultery by their marriage, save there has first been a true and contrite repentance, including restitution that has washed away the sin of the sinner.

81 Again, you know that the laws of old say that you shall make an oath to God before men to prove the seriousness of your intent.

82 But I say unto you: take no oaths to God before men to demonstrate your veracity or intent, but to men only say yes or no.

83 Let any oaths to Elohim only be for the purposes of Elohim, not for the purposes of man, and these only in private or within a close circle of your brothers and sisters of light.

84 You know that the laws of old say that there should be an eye for an eye and a tooth for a tooth. Yet have you ever known of a judge to demand an eye for an eye or a tooth for a tooth? No, not in all the history has it been so.

85 The meaning of this law then is that when an injury has been given by one to another, that the compensation to the injured must be equal to the injury suffered. No more or no less. And this is a true law of Elohim.

86 But not for all injuries does this apply, but only for those which cause a man grievous or irreparable harm to his life or income.

87 When grievances are more petty than grievous, let them be settled one man to another, one brother to another, one sister to another.

88 When petty disagreements and grievances cannot be settled brother to brother, then let there be a mediation of the family.

89 If the family decides the outcome, but one brother cannot abide the decision, let there be a mediation of those with that responsibility in the Family of Light,

and after hearing the facts and circumstances, let their decision be final.

90 Avoid the courts of law except for the most grave matters; those that are so grievous or have caused such irreparable harm that they cannot be reconciled by your family or the Family of Light.

91 Other than this, courts of law will inflict both the petitioner and the defendant with a poison to both their spirit and their life, from which they will not easily recover.

92 There are times when you will be burdened by the unreasonable actions or requirements of others. When these are in opposition to righteousness or of great seriousness, you should oppose them.

93 But often, they are merely an irritation, the acts of bullies and people in power. In such cases, it is better to affect indifference and even go beyond what is demanded, for then you take away their sport and they become bored and let you be.

94 Therefore, if a Roman comes and compels you to carry their pack for a mile, offer to carry it for two.

95 If a man slaps you in the face without cause, turn your other cheek to him as well, provided you or your family or the Family of Light are not threatened with real harm.

96 But if your family or the Family of Light is threatened, or your own life or safety, do as you must to defend yourself, but in that, do nothing that will make the matter worse.

97 If a man asks your help, turn him not away. And if a brother or sister asks to borrow that which you own,

let them have it as long you are not in need of it at that time and think not for its return until they either bring it back to you as a good steward should or you have need of it again.

98 You have heard in the laws of old that it is said to love your neighbors and to hate your enemies.

99 But I say unto you, hate not your enemies; love them as misguided children of God. Ask for blessings upon those that curse you that they might find the errors of their ways and do good deeds even for those that hate you, that their hate might be turned into admiration and respect.

100 Pray for those who spitefully use you or persecute you, that you might always be an example of the higher path walked by the Children of Light, who show by their lives that they are true sons and daughters of God.

101 Remember Elohim loves all the children of men and makes the sun to shine and the rain to fall for the blessing and benefit of everyone, both the good and the evil, the just and the unjust. Can you do any less than your Mother and Father in Heaven?

102 For if you only have love for those who love you, what could be your reward? For even the Publicans do the same.

103 And if you give greetings only to your brothers and sisters of light and ignore the wayward in the world, how are you any different than the Publicans or Pharisees, for do they not do the same?

104 Therefore, strive each day to be better in every way than the day before and strive each day to live your life in ways that are loving and virtuous and just, even

as Elohim is loving and virtuous and just with you, even in your imperfections.

105 Take heed that when you give alms, you do not do it before men to be seen. Do not sound a trumpet for the poor to gather and know that it is you who is their benefactor.

106 But when you give alms, do it in secret, that only those overseeing the largesse's may know from whence it came, and even then, if you give in anonymity, it is more pleasing unto God. And that which you do in secret shall be rewarded openly to you by Elohim.

107 When you give alms, do so without consideration for how much you are giving, except to be sure that it is not too little. Other than that, do not let your right hand, which gives alms, know how much your left hand took from your purse.

108 And when you pray, do not be as the hypocrites who love to pray long and tedious prayers, standing in the synagogues and on the corners of the streets so they may be seen by men. Verily, they shall have their reward, and it will not be what they think it will be.

109 But when you pray, go into a closet or a room where you are alone and shut the door that you can have privacy and pray to Elohim in secret as a friend speaks to a friend, and Elohim, who remains hidden from the eyes of men and is your truest friend, shall answer you openly.

110 When you are asked to publicly pray as a representative of your brothers and sisters, do so only in humility, with gratitude for the honor you have been given, and speak only with words that truly express the

feelings, desires, and beliefs of those who have called you to represent them before Elohim.

111 When you pray, except in prayers of sacred ritual, do not use vain repetitions as the heathen do, for they think that they shall be better heard by God for their many repetitions, but in fact, God hears them not, for their repetition shows that they pray only with their words and not with their hearts.

112 Verily, I declare to you: Elohim does not listen to the words of men said in prayers, except prayers that are said with feeling from the heart and with sincere love of God. To prayers other than this, God is deaf.

113 Understand that Elohim knows everything you are in need of before you ever ask. But by asking with passion and feeling from your heart and with sincere love for God, you demonstrate that you actually value that for which you ask.

114 When men sin against you and do not repent and confess to you and make restitution to you, you have no obligation to them.

115 But when men sin against you and are truly sorrowful for their action and offer a sincere repentance and honest restitution to you, then you must forgive them in full and remember their sins no more, even as Elohim forgives you in full and remembers your sins no more when you have given a sincere, full, and contrite repentance.

116 When you fast, do not be like the hypocrites who wear a sad countenance and stumble along that men may know they are fasting. Verily I say unto you they shall have their reward, and it will not be what they

think it will be.

117 But when you fast, make yourself clean and tidy, wear nice garments, have a smile on your face and warmth in your countenance that men may not even guess that you are fasting, unless they are fasting with you. And Elohim, who is in secret, shall reward you openly.

118 Lay not up for yourselves treasures upon the earth, where moth and rust decay and where thieves break through the gate and steal.

119 But lay up for yourselves treasures in Heaven, such as acts of kindness and love, of honesty and fidelity, and of goodwill and good stewardship, for these are the treasures which neither moths nor rust, or any of the plagues of men, can decay or corrupt. These are the treasures which thieves cannot break in and steal.

120 These are the treasures of enduring value, which mark you as a man among men in life and a prince among princes in the world to come.

121 The love of money and power are the Gods of the world and if you pursue and lust after either, let it be a warning that you have strayed from the path of Celestine Light.

122 For you cannot serve two masters; you cannot serve money or power and Elohim; either you will hate one and love the other or favor one and deny the other or hold to one and despise the other.

123 You cannot be a Child of Light and also love and avidly pursue money or power, for they are oil and water to one another and cannot mix, and only one can be first in your priorities.

124 But what shall become of you if you do not pursue money? Fear not; do what you love, and trust in God. Verily, I say unto you: do not be anxious about what you shall eat or what you shall drink or how you shall clothe yourself.

125 Be content with less, not working endlessly for more, for life is more than food and drink and the clothes you wear. It is more than the house you live in or the men that you command.

126 Life is meant to be lived in tranquility and joy, and these come from contentment with less, not always seeking more of the things of the world.

127 Fulfillment and happiness come from quiet days with your wife or husband, playing with your children, listening to the concerns of your brothers and sisters of light, being of service to your community, being a good steward of the land and to all the creatures of the earth.

128 If you have all the treasures of the earth, but you have not these things, you are most destitute among men and a pauper in the world to come.

129 Behold the fowls of the air; they neither sow nor reap, nor gather into homes, yet Elohim feeds and cares for them. If Elohim so loves the birds of the air and cares for their needs, how much more are you loved and cared for?

130 Why do you worry about tomorrow? Sufficient is the day for itself. Which of you by worrying or planning for a tomorrow that may never come can add one day to his life?

131 Verily, in worrying and working for the tomorrow that may never come, you sacrifice the day that is in

your hand.

132 In that sacrifice, you lose more than a day; you lose the moments with those you love that never were and prevent the moments that would have been from ever becoming.

133 And why do you worry about the clothes you wear? Consider the lilies of the fields, how they grow; they toil not, neither do they spin.

134 Yet I say unto you even King Solomon in all his glory was not arrayed like one of these.

135 Wherefore, if God so adorns the flowers of the field, which are here today, but wither tomorrow, and are cast into the oven, shall not Elohim so clothe you, O you children of little faith?

136 Therefore, take no thought, saying, 'what shall we eat or what shall we drink, or where shall we live, or how shall we be clothed?'

137 After all these things, those who are lost seek and sacrifice their lives for emptiness.

138 But Elohim knows you have need of all of these things, and if you do not pursue them foremost in your thoughts and actions, but instead store up for yourselves treasures in Heaven, then all these things shall come to you as you have need.

139 Like the birds of the air and the flowers of the fields, look to the earth to provide your needs, from the food you eat to the clothes you wear, to the homes you live in, to the money you need to buy little pleasures.

140 The earth has been given to you that you may have all of these things and have them in abundance, if you have faith; seek that which you desire to find, do

not expect it to simply fall out of the sky, and remain balanced in your life between your needs and your desires.

141 Therefore, do not live today for tomorrow, but live today for today. The days to come will have their own challenges. When living a life of peace, joy, and true fulfillment, sufficient is each day for the challenges therein.

142 Do not condemn others for their lifestyles and choices that are different from yours and do not despise those who do not believe as you do or hold the same things of value.

143 The more you judge others, the more they will reciprocate and judge you. And with the disdain that you show, so shall you be disdained.

144 Be careful not to speak with critical words or critical inflection in your voice to members of your family or your brothers and sisters of light, if they have not asked for your critical opinion.

145 Every fault you see in them, you likely have even greater in yourself, and only because of that can you recognize it in others.

146 Therefore, rather than criticize your brothers or sisters by word or even inflection or even by what you may think is a friendly suggestion, seek first to improve yourself and wait for them to seek out your opinion if they desire it.

147 When your brother or sister is ready for help, they will ask for your opinion or advice; therefore, a suggestion unasked for, that does not seek to improve without judgment, but first belittles by word or

inflection, are words that should never be spoken.

148 When you desire to praise another, shout it from the hilltop, but when you think to criticize another, chew upon your tongue.

149 Give not that which is holy to the dogs; neither cast your pearls before swine, lest they trample them under their feet and turn again and rend you.

150 Each day, there are only so many hours, and in your life, only so many days. Therefore, every day is precious and should not be squandered, trying to help those who do not desire your help or teach those who do not desire to be taught or uplift those who prefer to stay in the pit.

151 Be of good service, but only to those who value the time you give, only to those who seek the help you offer, only to those who desire to hear the good news you speak, and only to those who wish to be tomorrow more than they are today, not in the ways of the world, but in the ways of the Celestine Light.

152 Ask with faith, with selflessness, for anything of righteousness that is a need of in your life, and it shall be given to you. Seek with faith for anything of merit, and you shall find it. Knock with faith upon any door where you need to enter, and it shall open unto you.

153 For every person of virtue, who asks with faith, with selflessness, shall receive, and every person of virtue who seeks with faith shall find and every person of virtue who knocks with faith will find all doors open unto them.

154 Which one of you, if your son asked for a loaf of bread, would instead give him a stone?

155 Or if he asked for a fish, would instead give him a snake?

156 If you who are with faults still know how to give good gifts to your children, how much more shall our Father and Mother in Heaven, who are without fault, give good things to the Children of Light that ask of them?

157 Therefore, all the good things whatsoever that you wish men would do for you, do you even so for them; verily, this is the fruit of the law and the prophets.

158 I have spoken often of the Children of Light, and many here have wondered who they are and if they are one.

159 Verily, the Children of Light care not for the ways of the world, but are enraptured with the ways of Celestine Light and the Community and Family of Light. They walk a different path than the path of the world, a path that leads them to peace and fulfillment and community in this life and overwhelming joy, exaltation and expansion in the life to come.

160 A Child of Light comes not by birth or by decree, but by choice and the conviction to follow the precepts of Celestine Light they know to be true, because both their heart and their mind say it is so, and their prayers confirm it.

161 Many are called to be Children of Light, but few are chosen because only those who tend the orchard are allowed to harvest the fruit.

162 Many have not been called, but are still chosen because having seen the Celestine Light, they make the choice to abandon the darkness and live the light.

Like a wayward son, they are welcomed into the arms of Elohim.

163 If you would be a Child of Light, enter in at the strait gate, for wide is the gate and broad is the way that leads to destruction; and many are those that go that way.

164 But strait is the gate, and narrow is the way, which leads to life in the Celestine Light, and few are those that find it.

165 Beware of false prophets, for there shall be many that shall spread like a plague upon the land. They will come to you in sheep's clothing, but inwardly, they are ravenous wolves.

166 Everyone who preaches in my name is not of me, but only those who live the teachings of Celestine Light that I have given.

167 Words are like dust; alone they are worthless. It is only when someone speaks the teachings I have taught and their words are proven with actions of love, and service, and humility, and virtue, and respect, and stewardship that you may begin to accept that they are from me and true emissaries of the Celestine Light.

168 It is not by miracles that you will know them, but by knowledge that works miracles.

169 It is not by wealth that you will know them, but by austerity, that they give their excess above their needs to the poor.

170 It is not by having many men to command that you will know them, but by seeing them toiling by the sweat of their brow in common with their brothers and sisters of the community.

171 It is not by power that you will know them, but by a tenderness and stewardship for all life.

172 It is not by great oratory that you shall know them, but by the teachings of the Celestine Light they demonstrate with the example of their kind and virtuous life.

173 It is not by the deference that men give them that you shall know them, but by the respect and attentiveness they give to others, especially those of little means or position.

174 Therefore, though false prophets shall abound, there is no need for you to be led astray. Look to the things which I have given, by which you may separate the false prophet from the true. Then go in private and ask God to confirm the conclusions of your mind and the feelings of your heart.

175 Simply remember that you will know them by their fruits and that the life they live is a greater witness of their veracity than any of the words they speak.

176 Remember, you shall know them by their fruits. Do men gather grapes from the thorn bushes or figs from the thistles?

177 Every good tree brings forth good fruit, in harmony with the teachings of Celestine Light I have given and the life I have shown to you. But a corrupt tree brings forth fruit that does not come from the vineyard and orchard of Elohim, and it is fit only to be discarded upon the ground to rot.

178 Now some will say that they receive a little good fruit from the teachings of a false prophet, and therefore, they just ignore the words which have no harmony in

their heart and lift themselves up with the words that do.

179 But I say unto you that every good tree brings forth only good fruit. There is not a good tree that has one branch that bears sweet fruit and an adjacent branch that bears rotten fruit. And when fruit is gathered into a basket one bad fruit will spoil the basket, even as a single bad influence can decay that which would otherwise have remained good.

180 A truly good tree cannot bring forth evil fruit; neither can a tree corrupted bring forth good fruit that is not already tainted with its demise.

181 Every tree that does not bring forth good fruit must be hewn down and cast into the fire, lest it taint the purity of that which is good.

182 Wherefore, remember this test of a prophet and of a Child of Light: By their fruits of their life, you shall know them.

183 But do not think that a Child of Light or even a prophet or an Apostle will never have fault or err in their personal choices or that a leader of the Communities of Light will never sin and be in need of repentance. If they were already perfect, they would be translated in the blink of an eye and be no more upon the earth.

184 But in the life they live, you see them live as I have shown you and taught you to live. Not as the world lives, but only as the Children of Light live.

185 Nor should you think that everyone that calls out to God or praises Elohim or who claims to be acting in the name of God will actually ever enter into the Kingdom of Heaven, but only those who live the life and

truly do the will of my Father and Mother in Heaven.

186 Many will say to me on that day, 'Lord, Lord, have we not prophesied in your name? Have we not cast out devils in your name and in your name done many wonderful works?'

187 Then I will profess to them, 'I never knew you; you spoke in assuming words, but you never prophesied for me; you cast out devils, but they only laughed, for you had no authority; you have done many good works in my name, but with vanity for your glory, not in humility for mine. Depart from me you that work iniquity.'

188 Therefore, whosoever hears my words and lives them, I will liken to a wise man who built his house upon a rock.

189 And the rain descended, and the floods came, and the winds blew, and his house did not fall, for it was founded upon a rock.

190 And everyone who hears my words and lives them not shall be likened unto the foolish man who built his house upon the sand.

191 And the rain descended, and the floods came, and the winds blew and beat upon his house, and it fell, and great was the fall of it."

192 And it came to pass that when Yeshua ceased to speak, the people were astonished at what they had heard him say, for he spoke doctrines that put down things they had believed and presented doctrines they had never heard.

193 But he spoke teachings that made sense and resonated in their hearts. He spoke as one with authority, not as one of the scribes. An aura of divinity spread over

them, emanating from him insomuch that his words pierced them that they had tingles throughout their body. And though many might choose to not heed the words they had heard, none could doubt the veracity of what he had spoken.

SERMON ON THE MOUNT

PART 2

Excerpted from the Oracles of Celestine Light: Vivus: Chapter 46

While Yeshua had been speaking, his Apostles had been sitting in a semicircle directly below him and the multitude sitting beyond them. But in the place closest to him sat four women, and the order in which they sat was meaningful.

2 Facing Yeshua, his wife Miriam sat on the left, which was Yeshua's right hand and the place of honor reserved always for her; beside her was Salome; Martha was next; and Miryam, his mother, beside her.

3 Throughout his discourse, the women held hands or linked arms or leaned against the woman beside them. This was common practice among Miriam, Martha, and Miryam, but Salome had purposely been included with them and, by Martha's request, sat between her and Miriam, that she would have no doubt that they accepted her as one of their family and held no animosities for her part in the death of Yochanan.

4 After Yeshua had stepped down to go to the company of his family, Cephas stood up on the pinnacle and announced to the multitude in a

loud voice, "We have been blessed by the teachings of Yeshua, Son of Light; surely, none have heard his words this day and not been pierced by their significance and inspired by their promise.

5 Yeshua has told me that he desires to still speak more this day, but first, as it is already well into the afternoon, let us all break for a meal. But please remain where you sit, and once Yeshua has finished eating, he will speak to us again."

6 Then after asking for silence and saying a short prayer of thanksgiving and blessing for the food they would all eat, Cephas stepped down and went to his family.

7 The people did as Cephas bade. As most had traveled from other areas and encamped around the Communities of Light, they had ample food with them, and those that had none found the strangers around them happily shared whatever they had.

8 When Yeshua was ready to ascend again the pinnacle, he informed Cephas, who went up to the pinnacle and announced to the multitude that Yeshua would now to speak to them again.

9 Once again, Cephas offered a prayer for the multitude, asking, "Elohim, God of the earth and all that is, thank you for this opportunity we have to hear the words of Yeshua, your Son of Light. Let our hearts be open to receive the Celestine Light that he brings and our heads be clear to understand his words. So let it be."

10 Then Cephas stepped down from the pinnacle and Yeshua stepped up. Looking over the multitude,

he said unto them, "I know many of you have come to Capernaum to see me because you have heard it said that I have healed people in miraculous ways, and you hope that I will heal you or a member of your family.

11 When I come down from the mount, I will walk among you, and you may reach out and lightly touch my garment, and those who are prepared shall be healed.

12 That you may know that it is not through me alone that the Celestine power of Elohim comes to heal, but through any of the Children of Light who have been given that authority; my wife Miriam, who is one of my Apostles, and Cephas, another, will also walk among you.

13 If you are ready to be healed, you have repented of your weaknesses and stand upright before men and God. If this be so, then simply touch our garments as we pass by and ask aloud with your words for Elohim to heal you. We are bridges of the Celestine Light, and if you are prepared in your heart, it will be as you desire and you shall be made whole."

14 At this revelation, the Apostles were surprised, all save Miriam and Cephas, for Yeshua had not spoken of this to any of them or taught them how they could be channels of the Celestine power of Elohim as he was.

15 Then Yeshua preached to the multitude, saying, "This will be an afternoon of miracles, but it will also be an afternoon of disappointment. Many will seek to be healed, but only some will obtain that which

they seek.

16 How can that be? Why would some be healed, but others not? Is it the fault of the healer? Are they not true channels of the Celestine Light of Elohim? Nay, that cannot be so, for there are some that will be healed, even of very great diseases and infirmities.

17 Have you ever wondered why Elohim even allows suffering and disease and infirmities at all?

18 Have you not seen at times when the pain of suffering is so great or the agony from the loss of a loved one; that a person will cry out in despair to God, asking why?

19 If there truly is a benevolent God in Heaven, a mother and father who love their children beyond measure, how could this God of all that is, with the power to make or destroy the earth and all the heavens above with a single command, allow such misery and suffering and pain to their children who walk the earth?

20 You would be less than honest with yourself if you did not admit that at times, such questions have passed through your thoughts.

21 Today you will have the answer to those questions. You may not like the answers. You may not accept the answers. But you will know the answers.

22 I tell you these things with the hope that in understanding the truth, even if at first you may not accept its reality, that you will accept it enough that it will begin to alter your habits and choices and will make a beneficial difference in your life.

23 It is taught by the priests and leaders of the faiths

of this land that God is an omnipresent, omnipotent, presence. God is referred to in our times in the masculine structure of speech, but only as a form of speech, and is not thought of as actually having a form of a man.

24 But in ancient times, God was not so considered. In ancient times, God was spoken of in the plural and in both the masculine and the feminine.

25 When next you are in the synagogue and they are reading from the scripture scrolls, ask them to read of the creation of the world.

26 In truth, much has been removed from the sacred scrolls that were originally written, and more has been removed than remains.

27 Why was much that was written removed? Because the scrolls as they were originally given by Elohim to the prophets were given from Elohim and the true understanding and implications of that are at odds with the teachings that men desire to hear.

28 The very nature of the name Elohim, by which God chose to be known to man, is plural in its composition. More importantly, it embodies both the masculine and feminine. Even in what remains of the tattered scriptures read in the synagogues, this name of God is used over two thousand times.

29 But it is almost always used in contradiction upon itself, and this was not done by they who originally wrote the scrolls, but by the scribes and priests who came after them and desired a different God, for it is employed as a singular and masculine title, but it is in fact, not only plural, but both male

and female, even as the true God of Heaven is.

30 I speak now from the same scrolls that still are read in the synagogues, and God said, 'Let us make man in our likeness and let them have dominion . . . '

31 And again, 'Behold the man has become as one of us . . . '

32 And again, 'Let us go down, and there confound their language, that they may not understand one another's speech.'

33 In these words, you see mankind was made in the image not of God, but Gods. They were made male and female in physical appearance like the physical appearance of God, one a male, one a female; a father and a mother, a part of the Elohim whom you worship.

34 Elohim is not a faceless aeon without substance or form as is taught today. Even the very text of the scrolls read in the synagogues record Moses speaking to Elohim, face-to-face. That there is no doubt that the scroll records an actual event and not a metaphor, the scripture concludes, as one man speaks to another.

35 Understand that Elohim is not a faceless aeon of the male persuasion. Nor is Elohim only one aeon as you have been led to believe, but many.

36 But the Elohim that is the creator of this world are three: the Father, the Mother, and the Son, who is your brother, for the eternal soul of each of you is a creation of our Father and Mother in Heaven.

37 And more than this, an Elohim is also what each one of you can become someday as you learn

and grow from your experiences and choices and become perfect.

38 And it is for this cause—to learn and grow and become more perfect—that you should be striving for every minute of your physical life upon the earth.

39 And it is for this cause—that you might learn and grow by your experiences and choices—that suffering is allowed to exist in your life and the life of every person, some to a very great degree.

40 There is no greater desire of your Father and Mother in Heaven than you should return to them in glory, and they wait with love to embrace you and welcome you home.

41 But you cannot return to a realm of perfection ruled by the Elohim, unless you are first more perfect.

42 You do not need to be perfect as the Elohim are, for you continue to expand for all eternity and you have forever to improve upon your perfection.

43 But you must grow beyond the bonds of the ways of the world; you must grow into the ways of the Elohim; and in that, you become greater than you are, greater than you began, and with a harmony that can live in the presence of the Elohim.

44 When you seek to understand the nature of Elohim and try to comprehend why suffering exists and why bad things happen, even to the most wonderful and righteous people, remember how you help your own children to become more than babes, in the same manner your Father and Mother in Heaven seek to help all of their children upon the earth.

45 You let your children experience their life. You teach them right from wrong, what can hurt them and what is good for them. You admonish them to be of good character and virtue.

46 They journey through life, and they never forget the teachings you gave to them, both by word and by example.

47 But until your teachings are confirmed by their own experiences and observations, they do not shape them into more than they were.

48 By the teachings of your words and the examples of your lives, you lay the foundation for the building upon which your children construct their lives.

49 But the building is not built until they can prove by their own experiences and observations that the foundation is true.

50 By this, they learn and they grow. Sometimes, they make mistakes, and even those confirm the foundation you built and help them to become more the next day than they were the day before, if they so choose.

51 And I say unto you that every day of life is a school, no matter your age, and each day, there are many tests; and each choice you make, be it big or small, is one.

52 Sometimes people, even well-intentioned and righteous people, make the wrong choices. They learn from the pain and the error of their ways. When the choice comes again, they hopefully choose wiser.

53 It is better to experience a little pain and

suffering for your short time in mortality to help you to walk a better path than to not have that incentive to walk in righteousness and condemn yourself by your poor choices to far greater pain and suffering for days without end in the life to come.

54 It is by this means—to experience the bad and the good, to make choices, both right and wrong, to have the opportunity each day to become better than you were the day before—that your sojourn in mortality is fulfilled, and you may pass beyond the shining gate and into the realm of the Elohim forevermore.

55 "Consider this now—when a man is born crippled, it is asked who sinned, he, or his parents, that he was thus born.

56 I say unto you that neither the man nor his parents sinned, for Elohim is a God of love and would never punish a newborn with any punishment, for any cause.

57 I know it is not taught thus among many, but when you consider the nature of Elohim, consider your own nature as parents. Let your heart feel how you would feel. Let your mind think how you would think.

58 Would you who love your children cripple them at birth to be punished for your sins, instead of you?

59 Nay, you who love your children, yet are mortal and imperfect, would beg Elohim to put an infirmity upon you, rather than see your child suffer. Do you think that your Father and Mother in Heaven, being immortal and perfect, could act any less loving or

caring for their children of spirit?

60 How then is it that a man is born crippled? Or another suffers from disease when he is a man? Or another, a lover of peace, is murdered at the hands of bandits? Or why is one man healed by a spiritual blessing, but another remains as he is?

61 One answer to all of these questions returns to the journey of mortality and what it is that each of you desired to gain in your sojourn upon the earth, as you contemplated the journey, before you were ever conceived in your mother's womb.

62 Verily, verily, I say unto you: Before you were born of woman, you were born of spirit, and before you lived upon the earth, you lived in spirit beyond the earth.

63 You came down into mortality that you could experience things that only a physical and mortal body can experience, and this that you might learn from your experiences; that you might become an eternal soul of greater wisdom, of more love, and fuller empathy and sympathy for your brothers and sisters of life and eternity.

64 That you might become more like the Elohim.

65 Therefore, when you see a man born crippled, do not imagine who sinned that he was thus born; do not scorn or pity him. Instead, honor him, for he has shown uncommon love for himself and his family and an intrepid courage and devotion of desire to grow into a magnificent Son of Elohim by being thus born.

66 Having lived within the challenges, he will gain

empathy and sympathy for the plights of others such as no one who has not lived thus can ever gain.

67 Having lived within the challenges, he will learn to cherish love, both that which he receives from others and that which he can give to them; and this in ways such as no one who has not lived thus can ever gain.

68 Having lived within the challenges, he will see all the world with different eyes and learn to appreciate the beauty and wonder of many common things, in ways such as no one who has not lived thus can ever gain.

69 Having lived within the challenges, he will afford his closest family and friends an opportunity to also learn empathy, and sympathy, and love, and stewardship to a greater degree than they otherwise would have been able, had he not been born thus and lived among them.

70 Therefore, when a person is born crippled, but still capable, this is someone who chose to be born thus, before they were ever birthed, that both they and their family and friends might have greater opportunities in their sojourn in mortality to become more than they began.

71 Sometimes an affliction will strike a man in the prime of his life, for no apparent cause of his own. But like the man born crippled, this can sometimes be a choice made before he was ever born into the world or a choice made by his higher spirit later in his life to help him or those in his life to learn greater empathy, sympathy, faith, and love.

72 But there is also a second aeon that may overshadow the man who becomes afflicted later in life, and it is this aeon that is usually the cause.

73 Like the man who was born crippled, it is often the case that the man who acquires a disease or infirmity also made the choice to do so. But unlike the man born crippled, he may not have made the choice by action, but by inaction or incorrect action.

74 There are certain laws of health by which you would be wise to abide. These are not necessarily laws written on the sacred scrolls, but they are taught and known to the Children of Light.

75 Living the true laws of health and vitality produce superior wellness. More pointed, not living the laws of health, whether by choice or ignorance, bring about greater disease and afflictions.

76 This body you wear is mortal. It is subject not only to death, but to all manner of diseases, infirmities, and imperfections. That is how it was created by Elohim that through your mortality, you would be given the opportunity to make wise choices.

77 As you are a good steward of the temple of your body, that habit becomes a part of who you are, and you become a better steward of other things given to your care such as your children, your animals, your crops, and your community.

78 As you prove yourself with lesser things, Elohim will give you greater things, both in this life and the next.

79 Elohim rewards the good steward, but has an

empty cup for the poor steward, save they recognize the error of their ways, repent, and commit to living a greater light.

80 Therefore, when you find yourself sick and afflicted, do not curse what has happened to you, but give thanks that through your infirmity you are reminded that you are the master of yourself and can make changes in your lifestyle that will improve the state of your wellness in the times to come.

81 If you do not learn the lesson of your poor health, even as you recover, you are doomed to fall to another infirmity soon again.

82 Therefore, this day, as I walk among you as a bridge of light between man and God, to bring the healing Celestine Light of Elohim upon you, reach out and touch my garment if you will; if you have the faith; if you have the desire; if you are dedicated to living the greater light called Celestine.

83 Consider the man who took off his garments and labored in a loin cloth for all of the day under the hot sun, because he was uncomfortable and sweating wearing his clothes.

84 At the end of the day, his body badly burned, he sought to be healed. He reached out to touch the light, but it did not come upon him and he was not healed, for it had been by his choice that he had forsaken his clothing that protected him from the sun, and he had not learned from his error, and upon another day, the same thing he would do.

85 Then there was the man who was imprisoned by the Romans and forced to work all day in the hot

sun in just his loin cloth. He too was badly burned; he too desired to be healed by the light; but when he reached out with faith and hope to touch the light, his body was restored as it had been, because the cause of his suffering had not been by his choice, and in his desire to be healed, he held humility and faith and love and desired to be a better man in his heart.

86 As I walk among you today, ask yourself which man are you: the wise man who seeks to ever act in wiser ways or the foolish man who seeks always immediate comfort and pleasure and considers not the painful consequences that shall fall upon him on the morrow."

87 Then Yeshua stepped down into the crowd, and he beckoned Miriam and Cephas to also come down into the multitude. And the three of them walked out in different directions that they might go among all of the people.

88 As they passed through the multitude, nearly everyone present reached out a hand to touch them, not just those who were noticeably infirmed or afflicted.

89 The old and the young, the Hebrew and the Gentile, the Egyptian and the Roman, all reached forth their hands and let them linger on their garments, with softness and respect, as they moved slowly among them.

90 And of miracles, there were many. Men on litters stood up and walked. People with sundry pains from sources they knew not suddenly had none. Men, women, and children who had been blind for years

or since birth at once saw the wonder of the world, and they fell to their knees and praised Elohim.

91 Many who had no noticeable affliction still were changed, and you could see it in their countenance, which as they touched Yeshua or Miriam or Cephas went from an expectant, hopeful smile to rapture and joy and tears.

92 Though some were not healed, as Yeshua had said would be so, upon the joyous faces of the thousands of people in the crowd, it could not be doubted that almost all had seen and felt a light such as they had never imagined, even the Celestine Light, and they would return to their homes with a warmth in their hearts that before had never been.

CHALLENGES OF LIFE AND ETERNITY

Excerpted from the Oracles of Celestine Light: Vivus: Chapter 48

Shortly thereafter, Yeshua was in the boat with
Cephas and Yohhanan while his family and
the other Apostles sat or stood along the
shoreline with the gathering crowd of people.
19 About the third hour after sunrise, Yeshua began
to speak to the multitude, saying, "Some of you have
been away from your homes for many days now, and it
is time for you to return.
20 Will you be the same person when you return as
you were when you left or will you be different?
21 My teachings are like seeds sown upon good soil.
Each of you is the good soil. You would not have come
here and remained here for these days if your hearts
were not beating to my words and your eyes not seeking
a greater light.
22 But when you return to your home, you become the
gardener of your life, which is your greatest stewardship.
For my seeds to grow and fill you with light, you must
wisely cultivate the garden of your life.
23 You are also the steward of many more things,
including your relationships, which can span eternity.

But unless you first are a good steward of your own life, unless you first cultivate and blossom the garden that bears your name, a good steward of anything else, you can never be.

24 What do you hope for in the days to come? What do you work and strive for? Are you caught in a rut upon the road of life? Do you see tomorrow as only another day of the same challenges and maybe more or as a new dawn, rising upon a new and better life?

25 To know the answer, you merely need to look at your life. If you return home and nothing is different with the way you think and speak and act, if your weaknesses are still your weaknesses and the friends who would lead you to temptation still beckon, then you remain upon the road you have always traveled. Today will be as yesterday and tomorrow as today.

26 But new seeds have been planted in your heart. They will grow into marvelous flowers of the sun if you will but cultivate and nourish them.

27 And how is this done? How do you cultivate the flowers of Celestine Light planted in your heart? With love and humility, with repentance and restitution, with respect and honesty, with service and prayer, with a life renewed as the old garden is turned under that the new garden may blossom.

28 Therefore, do not just hear my words and nod your heads in agreement, but hear my words and do them."

29 Then a man stepped to the lake shore from the crowd, and he was a zealot who had been standing with the Apostle Shim'on. And raising his voice, he spoke out to Yeshua, saying, "You speak of being a steward over

your own life and that is all well and good, but how can a man who is a slave be the steward over his own life or even a man who is not a slave, but under more subtle bondage as a citizen of a Kingdom ruled by a tyrant king?"

30 Yeshua answered him, saying, "Thank you for your question, Garz-el. You have well introduced that which I desired to speak upon."

31 The man was startled to hear Yeshua call him by name, and in surprise, he asked, "How did you know my name? We have never met or spoken."

32 Yeshua answered him, saying, "A shepherd knows his sheep, even as the sheep know their shepherd. When a new sheep joins the flock, he does not need to be shown to the shepherd to be known by him, any more than the shepherd needs to be introduced to the sheep to be able to single him out from among the flock.

33 Even a slave can be a steward over themselves. The master may dictate where the slave must go and what he must do, what he must wear, and what he must eat and drink. But the master cannot dictate what the slave will think, nor hear his prayers to Elohim, or know the true desires of his heart.

34 In all things, Elohim expects the best you have to offer of yourself, but does not expect more than you can give, even as the slave who is a good steward over his thoughts and prayers and desires, but is not held accountable for the food or drink he is compelled to consume by his master or the clothes he must wear or the things he must do.

35 And woe unto the master who compels his slave

to do evil or to the officer of the army who compels his soldiers to initiate attacks against the peaceful instead of only protections and defense against the marauders, or to the rulers of Kingdoms who compel the innocent to evil, who would otherwise be pure.

36 For them, it would almost be better that they had never been born, for when one man forces another to sin, where to object would be death or great penalty, that man takes upon him the sins of they who were compelled, and the penalties in the hereafter shall be multiplied seventy times upon that man.

37 And though a man of darkness may compel one of light to commit evil and may escape a penalty in this life, know that it is only for a breath of eternity, and in the hereafter all shall be held accountable for the actions of their lives for much longer than a breath.

38 In the hereafter, each person's light and darkness shall be weighed in the balance, and they who are found wanting shall be cast out into outer darkness, into the place of torment which they created in life, and are pulled to in the life to come by their own resonance.

39 And in that prison of their making, there shall be great weeping and wailing and gnashing of teeth, until they have paid the utmost and redeemed themselves.

40 In outer darkness, the evil will burn; every part of them inside and out shall feel as if fire is eating at them, but they will never be consumed; always burning, but never scorched, in the flames, but without light, but also in utter cold, in impenetrable darkness and loneliness without solace.

41 And it is not by Elohim that their torment comes,

but only by their own hand by the resonance they created by their thoughts and actions in their previous life.

42 Before the world ever was, Elohim laid out the plan by which all things would be, not just in this life, but also in the life to come.

43 And to all the thoughts of man, there would be an accounting. And to all the actions of man, there would be an accounting. And the accounting is written upon the resonance of your soul.

44 Good thoughts and deeds are credited with light upon your soul. Wicked thoughts and deeds bring darkness to your soul.

45 Once your last breath in mortality is taken, your soul will rise at once to a place of judgment, or so it is thought. But in reality, this is but a house of measures.

46 Your soul is put into a balance, and the light and the darkness which you put into it in mortality are weighed one against the other until your place of resonance is determined.

47 And there you are sent, not by force or decree, but by the inexorable pull of your own soul toward its resonance, the dark to the darkness and the light to the light.

48 The difference is in this life; you may sin and not only feel no pain or consequences from your actions, but might even feel pleasure in your sin. But in the eternity to come, you cannot escape the consequences of your darkness.

49 If your balance is found wanting, you will be pulled by the resonance you created in life, into the outer

darkness.

50 The greater your darkness in life, the deeper into outer darkness you will be drawn; and the deeper into outer darkness you fall, the greater the pain that never ends will wrack you and torment you, and the fire that burns but never consumes will torture you.

51 Knowing this, a man should consider well before he compels another to sin, for the darkness of the sin is multiplied seventy times upon the head of the man who compels or seduces another to do evil.

52 How much greater then will be the weight of the darkness of his soul when it is weighed in the balance?

53 But even as the soul of a man can be drawn into outer darkness in eternity because of his sins in this life, so can the soul of a man be drawn into greater light, even into the presence of the Elohim by the weight of the light in his soul from the good thoughts and deeds of his sojourn in mortality.

54 The same man who owns a slave and has compelled him to do evil can free his slave and ask forgiveness of his slave by word and make restitution by deed. In this, great light comes into his soul and puts away the darkness.

55 The same commander who ordered his men to attack a city whose people had not attacked them could, when given the choice again, refuse to so act. In the future, helping to build instead of destroy, he could bring light to his soul instead of darkness.

56 The same king who ruled his people unjustly and compelled them to act against their light could repent and ask forgiveness of his people and then prove the

value of his words by his good deeds; thus where before his soul drew darkness unto it, now it would draw light.

57 It is never too late to turn from darkness to the light. But you know not which day and hour your soul shall be called from this life to make an accounting for eternity. Therefore, do not procrastinate or delay to think, act, and live in the Celestine Light.

58 Your eternity awaits you, and whether you live in a world of light and joy and abundance or a world of darkness and cold and hunger depends entirely upon the choices you make every moment of every day, for you are the architect and builder of your forever."

FAMILY

Excerpted from the Oracles of Celestine Light: Vivus: Chapter 50

The next day, on the Sabbath, the Children of Light, both the old and the young, from all of the Communities of Light along Lake Gennesaret, met together at Capernaum for edification, one with another, as was the custom on that day.

18 Shortly afterward, Yeshua came up to the rise and spoke to the Children of Light, saying, "Words cannot express the happiness I feel because of the joy of these women whom I love and am honored and blessed to call my wives.

19 You look to me to guide and teach you in the ways of the Celestine Light of Elohim, and that is one of my great purposes upon the earth in mortality. But even as you, I experience light every day, and I learn and am uplifted by the light that comes upon me.

20 Each of you brings light into my life. Witnessing your victories each day over the adversary within; seeing your own growth in the Celestine Light, how each day you strive and most often succeed at becoming better than you were; seeing how you teach your children with love and tenderness and by honest example—these things and so many more uplift and inspire my spirit

every day.

21 But it is within the walls of our own home, within the embrace of our own wives and children or husbands as it may be, that we truly glorify one another and help our dearest loved ones to transcend the bonds of mortality in spirit, even while we are still in this physical life.

22 So it is with my wives and children.

23 To marry with love, to have children, and to share an unbreakable bond and devotion to one another—this is a great part of the Plan of Eternal Progression that Elohim laid out before the world ever was.

24 It is with your family that you are called to do your greatest work for Elohim. Though you may be a busy man of commerce or called to be an Apostle and carry great demands upon your time or called to be a missionary far from your family for a time, you must never neglect your family.

25 Your family, and love itself, is like the most delicate and beautiful of flowers. It requires constant devotion and attention to thrive, and when it thrives, it brings you a joy and fulfillment as great as anything you will ever experience.

26 Do you desire to truly know Elohim? Do you wish to feel the endless and boundless love that your Father and Mother in Heaven have for you? Then embrace the companions of love with whom you journey through eternity, not just in passing, but hold them tight, listen to their breathing, and feel their heart beat against yours. Smell the sweetness of their hair and feel the softness of their skin.

IN THE WORLD BUT NOT OF IT

Excerpted from the Oracles of Celestine Light: Vivus: Chapter 52

Yeshua continued to speak to the brothers and sisters of the Communities of Light, saying, "I exhort you now, my brothers and sisters of light, to always set yourselves apart from and above the world.

2 As you grow in numbers and talents of the members of the communities, seek to become self-sufficient in your most basic needs, that though you may know of the world, you will not be dependent upon it, or in debt to it, or under threat of the vacillations and pettiness of its leaders.

3 Be always proficient in the making of homes and boats and all things such as you have need of in your daily lives.

4 Let each brother who has a skill teach it to many other brothers of the community, and let each sister who has a skill teach it to many other sisters of the community.

5 There will always be both necessities and gifts that you will purchase from the merchants of the world, but as much as it is possible with your numbers and talents, provide for yourselves the things in which you are in need.

6 Strive with diligence to have bounty and excess far beyond your needs, that you may store some for days of famine and pestilence that will surely come.

7 It will be well with you if all of the things which you eat and drink come from your own hands, from fruits and vegetables you have planted, harvested, and collected wild from the bounty of the earth, from fish you have caught and sea plants you have gathered, from honey you have fetched from the bees, and from all manner of foods you have prepared from the things you have brought unto you.

8 Food, shelter, clothing, and a means to earn a livelihood—in these things, let the Communities of Light become as self-sufficient as your numbers and talents and resources will allow.

9 The greater your self-sufficiency, the more you will be above the world and beyond the reach of its poisons, with the opportunity every day to live a life of happiness, joy, and fulfillment.

10 But the less self-sufficient you are, the more you will be within the grasp of the evil and people of the world insomuch that your life will often be darkened by the clouds of the world, the storms thereof which only bring pain, suffering, broken lives, and lost dreams.

11 The things you eat and drink must be of great importance to you. As you grow as a Child of Light, you learn which foods and drinks benefit your body and which do not.

12 As many of the foods and drinks of the world bring darkness into your body instead of light, it is far better if all of your food and drink comes only from those things

which you have grown, caught, gathered, and prepared yourself.

13 Let the wine you drink also only be from your vineyards and orchards, from fruits you have grown and harvested and made into wine.

14 Let not your wine be defiled with excessive spirits that befuddle the head, but let it be like Tiyrosh of the pure fruits—sweet to the taste, slight of spirits, invigorating to the body, and calming to the restlessness of man.

15 Let Celestine wine be of two types—that of normal consumption which is like sweet water and should contain not more than three parts per hundred of the spirits to help preserve its freshness and purity, and that of celebrations and holidays which may contain up to five parts per hundred but is limited to one cup each day of the holiday or celebration, and then shared only within the privacy of your homes among friends and family in a salutation of inspiration.

16 And make no excuses for a second cup or a large cup that is in reality more than one. For that is the way of the world where one cup leads to another until drunkenness and defiling of the temple occurs. But be Celestines as you have been called—honoring your temples and master of yourselves.

17 Of the wines of the world, drink not at all, save in a most dire need, and then only Tiyrosh and never Shekar or any other type of strong drink on any occasion.

18 Only with the wine you make with your own hands, grown from grapes in your own vineyards, and fruits in your own orchards, can you depend on to be pure and

of light, free from the poisons and errors that men of the world might put upon that which they make, be it intentionally or unintentionally.

19 Let this be an endeavor of the Communities of Light that Celestine wine shall become known among the world for its purity and deliciousness insomuch that even Caesar and the priests shall come unto you for an elixir of heaven.

20 Listen now, brothers and sisters, for I have another thing of great importance to share with you. Even now as you build the Communities of Light around Lake Gennesaret, you must begin preparing for the days when you shall depart from this land, never to return.

21 For there shall come great tribulations upon all the land of Palestine because of the Romans, and when those days come, the Children of Light must be no more in this place.

22 Therefore, begin preparing for your departure, not to one place alone, but to a few places upon the world where you can take root in peace upon the land and let your light shine forth upon it, until the days when the pull of the world can no longer hold the righteous and virtuous, and they shall be changed in the twinkling of an eye from mortality to immortality and rise to meet me in the sky.

23 Some will go into the sanctuary of the mountains, and others shall be children of the sea. Still others will dwell at the very heart of the world and be unseen.

24 While you are still nurtured in the communities of Gennesaret, become learned in skills that will serve you well, both in the community and upon the far places of

the world. By this, even when you are living among the Ganish, you will be respected for your abilities, virtue, and character.

25 With the gifts given to you as Children of Light by Elohim, while you are still upon the earth in mortality, you are called to be stewards of the land and all the creatures therein and healers of both animals and people, both among the Children of Light and among those of the world who are lost, but still of virtue and righteousness, looking for a greater light to guide their lives.

26 When you depart the communities of Lake Gennesaret, see that you remember and continue to live the principles of life you have learned here, that your light will kindle the fire of truth in others to whom it shall touch, until the day comes when you are called together again to travel home to the greatest light and to your reward as faithful Children of Elohim.

27 Whether you become part of those who form a Community of Light on an isle of the sea, or in a land afar, or in the heart of the lands of the Ganish, see that you keep alive all of the things I have taught you, especially about your gifts and callings and the exclusivity of your food and drink from that of the world and the importance of self-reliance and self-sufficiency, leaning only upon your fellow brothers and sisters of light, and not upon the world.

28 Teach these precepts to your children and admonish them to teach them to their children and on unto the last generation for those who remain behind by their choice, when most will depart to their glory. By

seeing these precepts lived, it shall be a way by which one Child of Light shall recognize another when they first encounter one another in lands far away.

29 For in the days to come, new Children of Light shall come down to the earth from the Celestine Light, sprinkled like celestial rain upon the earth, born into families of many cultures, races, and religions. Many will never have seen another Child of Light before they meet you or those who remain behind to hold the light.

30 Regardless of the color of their skin or their culture or class or the religion they may profess, by the light of their life you shall know them, and by the wonder of your light, which will resonate in their heart, they shall recognize you.

31 And there are those who become Children of Light as they live their lives and make good choices despite the darkness that may surround them.

32 They too will shine in a way unlike all others around them, and you may know them by their light, and they will know you by yours.

33 Let them gather unto you that they may leave the dreariness and darkness and discover the Family of Light and be one with the light that their brilliance may come forth.

34 For whether a Child of Light came from Heaven and held true to their essence despite the adversity of the world or came upon the earth without light, surrounded by darkness, but by choices of virtue and nobility became a Child of Light, in the eyes of Elohim, they are one and the same.

35 I would speak to you now somewhat of miracles

and healing.

36 When those who only see with the eyes of the world see a miracle, it seems like magic to them because they do not understand the well from which it issues.

37 When the blind see, or the lame walk, or the storm is stilled, or the food is multiplied, or any other miracle that you may see or do is accomplished, it is not by some magic power, as it would seem to the eyes of the world, but by an understanding and adherence to immutable laws of Elohim that permeate all of nature, even the very air we breathe.

38 A person of the world, even one without education, thinks that they understand the law of the attraction of the earth that if something is dropped, be it a stone or a beam, it falls to the ground.

39 But they do not understand, nor can they learn in any school, that there is also the law of the attraction of the sky, whereby the stone upon the ground may fly up into the air. Someday, men will learn of this law, but it is given to the Children of Light today to understand every natural law by which Elohim governs all things.

40 Therefore, when you command a stone to rise off the ground and fly through the air, it will seem as if you are endowed with magical powers to the people of the world, but in truth, you are merely Children of Light, utilizing laws of Elohim, unknown to the world, but known to you, because to the faithful, Elohim shares all the secrets of Heaven.

41 As Children of Light, you are blessed to learn the secrets and mysteries of Heaven. Anything you have seen or heard that I have done, you also can do, and

much more than that, as you learn and understand the laws of all creation, given by Elohim.

42 The mystery of all things I shall teach to my Apostles, and they shall teach to the faithful, one step at a time. Do not seek to learn of the greater powers until you have mastered the lesser, for it is by mastery of the lesser that the great powers can be manifested.

43 Now I would speak to you concerning health and longevity and healing of the sick and afflicted, for unless you have an understanding of these things, you will always be blocked in your understanding of greater things.

44 In all things, you reap what you sow, and concerning how long you shall live or how robust your health shall be while you live, these things are like the miracles I spoke of; they are governed in many ways by immutable laws laid down upon all creation by Elohim. They who know the laws sow in understanding and reap accordingly, and great is the harvest.

45 Now it is taught in the synagogues and in many of the religions of the world that the days of man are numbered by Elohim, but this is not so. The end is written not in the stars, but in daily choices people make for life or death. The number is known to Elohim, but set by the choices made by man.

46 Though death can come suddenly and unexpectedly by accident or war, it most often comes in a thousand bites of poison that slowly sap the health and life of even the man of strongest vigor.

47 Now Elohim sees the number of days of man upon the earth, not because they were numbered by Elohim,

but because they have been numbered by man by his choices of health and vigor, and seeing this, Elohim knows when the end shall come upon the man.

48 But the ways of man can change, and in saying this, know that I include women and children too. If a man continues upon the path of health he walks, be it good or bad, Elohim knows when his end shall come upon him.

49 But when the man changes a bad habit for a good, a poor choice for a better, the days he has numbered upon the earth increase, and Elohim then sees the days to come that were not there before.

50 It is given unto you to understand how to utilize faith and call upon the powers of Heaven for healing the sick and afflicted, but I exhort you to be prudent in the use of this gift of knowledge, ability, and faith.

51 All the people of the world and many of the Children of Light are afflicted with diverse afflictions and diseases that cause them pain and suffering and shorten their life. Should you spend your days healing all of these people?

52 Better it would be to spend your days teaching them the ways of health and longevity as revealed by Elohim unto the faithful that by better choices, many of the people could heal themselves.

53 And what shall you do when a man who is afflicted comes to you begging for a healing, and your heart beats in sympathy with his because of his pain? Or the man who is dying and offers to give you his fortune if you will just give him more days upon the earth? Or when one such as this is, a friend or a member of your family

whom you love greatly?

54 Verily, I say unto you: It is your obligation as a son or daughter of light and love to use the knowledge and powers that have been given to you to heal all those who are ready to be healed, who call upon you and Elohim, be they a Child of Light or a confused wanderer in the world.

55 But for those not ready to be healed, even among the Children of Light, you have no obligation, nor should you heal them, even from compassion, save it be for a greater glory of Elohim.

56 Who then is ready to be healed? Always those who are of good heart and character and have proven by their actions a commitment to live the greater laws of health and vigor and longevity as given by Elohim, also those who strive to live in the light and whose affliction was not caused by their choices, but simply by adversity.

57 This may sound to be without compassion, but it is truly said with the greatest of love and desire to see all be in health and wellness.

58 Your greater task is not to heal the afflicted, but to teach the afflicted better ways to live, that their afflictions will be no more.

59 When a man does not love himself enough to treat his body like a temple, as Elohim has asked, he dishonors both himself and Elohim.

60 To heal the afflicted of pain and suffering caused by their own choices before they have shown a commitment to the higher path of health is to squander your time and talents upon something you will not change except for a moment in time.

61 For a time, the afflicted will be healed by your blessing and the healing may even be momentous. But unless the person was changed in their heart to a higher path of health before you healed them, they will continue on the path that led to their infirmity, and their end will still be a destruction of their temple, despite all that you did.

62 Consider the fisherman who, thinking himself cunning, sought to slip among the crocodiles of the river Nile to catch a great fish, but instead was caught in the jaws of many teeth. Staggering back to safety, he sought a Child of Light to restore his arm torn asunder.

63 Once healed, he thought to himself still of the great fish and, vowing to be even more cunning, sought it once more among the crocodiles, and this time, lost not just his arm, but his life.

64 Of what good then was the healing upon his arm if in his heart he had not changed? Without first a change of heart, the healing is not esteemed, Elohim is not glorified, and the man's fate is not averted, merely delayed.

65 Therefore, even if it is your own wife or husband upon the sickbed, let the sickness run its course, unless they have shown by word and deed and the truth of the vision of their aura that they are committed to the higher course of health as given by Elohim, and if that is so, heal them quickly.

66 If it is not, love them, teach them, and help them to be stronger in their will than they have been. But do not heal them until they have proven commitment to the path that will banish sickness and afflictions that come

only because of their own slackness in obedience to the laws of health as given by Elohim.

67 With children who are afflicted, use your wisdom and give your love. Because of their youth, they may not yet fully understand the consequences of their actions and may become sick or afflicted in ignorance.

68 Therefore, when their life is not in danger from their sickness, let it be upon them just a bit so they learn the pain of poor choices, then heal them quickly that they learn the power of Elohim through the hands of the righteous, endowed with the knowledge of the workings of all things.

69 And what are the laws of life and health you must teach? To keep the Twelve Commandments of Sinai, to breathe good air and drink good water that is clear and flowing and abounding in life.

70 To eat the foods you have been taught to eat is of the greatest of importance to your health and longevity, as are the habits of cleanliness that you keep.

71 In that regard do not keep domestic animals in your home and let the place of sleep, even for pets, be beyond the threshold, except for those that are tiny, and leave no fur or waste amidst the places you dwell.

72 Wash your body often with herbs of cleansing and your hands more so, even every time you touch anything unclean and always before you prepare or eat your food.

73 You need to be outside often with vigorous movements of your body, sweating sometimes and drinking in sunshine over every part of your bare skin.

74 Therefore, if you are a Child of Light, do not be ashamed of your nakedness, for thus were you made by

Elohim that you might be blessed by the healing light of the sun and invigorated by the depth of its warmth. But suffer not those who lust upon those so revealed to see their glory. And if the lustful cannot repent and overcome themselves, suffer them not to remain among you.

75 Among all the creatures that roam the land, it is man whom Elohim has blessed with a scarcity of hair that their bare skin might more readily absorb the healing light and warmth of the sun than any other of Elohim's creations. For this cause, nudity in the sun for a short time each day should be common and encouraged among the Children of Light.

76 But you must be ever vigilant in both yourself and others of lust outside of the sacredness of marriage. If anyone sees another in nakedness to whom they are not married, of whom they have thoughts of lust, let them not be in their presence. If this requires separation of the sexes when naked, and by sexual inclination, so must it be, but only if you cannot look upon one another simply with admiration and without lust.

77 For your thoughts are the foundations of your actions. When your thoughts are pure, so shall your life be in virtue. But if your thoughts are impure, so shall your actions become defiling.

78 And for health and longevity, your thoughts are also of great importance. Good humor and good thoughts birth long life, while a sour disposition brings about an early death and much misery along the way.

79 Cultivate a love for one another that is deep and abiding insomuch that even beyond the family under

your roof, you have a love that is felt in your heart for each of your brothers and sisters of light in the community so much so that whatsoever they should ask of you that is righteous and within your power to grant, you will give it to them with joy and gratitude to be able to help someone you love.

80 And in that channel, find service to one another and to your community. Even as you love one another, love your community, for it is a part of you and you are a part of it.

81 Any good thing therefore that you can do in the service of your brothers and sisters of light or your community is pleasing unto Elohim, warming to your heart, and enlarging upon your soul.

82 Remember to be balanced in all things and gracious, not judgmental in your toleration of the weaknesses of others. Seek first to perfect the temple of your own life before you judge others about theirs.

83 With balance and nonjudgment, see that you also have no grudges or grievances among you, for such become the wedge that splits the rock.

84 If one of you find a wedge coming between you and another member of the community, first go to them and seek a resolution of peace and with love.

85 If you cannot find this harmony, then go together to the patriarch or matriarch and seek their wisdom.

86 If you still cannot find harmony one with another, go to the Council of Eleven and seek their advice.

87 If you still cannot find harmony, let the council pass a binding judgment to settle the matter and let they who were at odds with one another find a place of peace and

love and harmony with the judgment of the council.

88 If one or both cannot find such a place in their hearts, that their disagreement can be forgiven and forgotten, let them leave the community; else, they become the wedge that splits the rock.

89 Understand that all of these things of which I have spoken concerning health and longevity and peace and love and harmony are not commandments but admonishments.

90 You will not be punished by Elohim if you do them not, but will only be punishing yourself with greater sickness and afflictions and life and community challenges when you do them not.

91 Now I would speak to you of joy and revelry, for there should be much of it in the Communities of Light. Let music by instruments and songs ring forth in the communities from many places, from the women in the kitchen to the man upon the sea; let there be songs and whistling and humming and rhythm and harmony of voice with others.

92 Let everyone learn to play an instrument even if only to beat a stick upon a pot. And let music be heard often in the communities, both when alone and with many.

93 Now Elohim is the great creator of all that is, and wondrous are the beautiful creations of Elohim. But you are children of Elohim, and the ability to create works of beauty and wonder also resides within each of you.

94 Therefore, let everything in the community be done with beauty and creativity so that it is pleasing to the eye as well as of function. When you cast a pot, do

not simply make a pot, but give it symmetry and adorn it with patterns and designs.

95 When you make a simple gate, do not merely make it with branches laid side by side, but weave them into a pattern of beauty and wonder.

96 When you make a boat to catch the fishes of the sea, do not merely make a boat like all the other fishermen, but create designs upon it, not necessarily with function, but some simply for beauty and artistry.

97 When you lay your food upon the table, do not simply heap it into a bowl, but present it like a flower with patterns and colors that are pleasing to the eye.

98 When you build your house, do not build it plain or exactly like your neighbor, but let it be an expression of you and show creativity in design and color, with artistic accents abounding.

99 When you seek to give a gift to your husband or wife or child, do not simply buy a piece of cloth or a hook for fish or give them an extra bowl of dates, but create something by your own hands with love and artistry, be it functional or just for beauty, that they may have a piece of you with them every time they use it or gaze upon it.

100 Verily, you are the chosen children of Elohim. You are blessed to learn of and know all the mysteries of Heaven: to be able to live in the world but not be of it; to have joy, prosperity, peace, health, and long life, such as the world cannot even imagine.

101 Therefore, remember always who you are, be worthy of yourself and of the great blessings Elohim has given unto you. Live always in the light. Be ever

the noble princes and princesses of Heaven; it is your blessing to become as you fulfill the full measure of your creation."

the noble princes and princesses of Heaven. It is your blessing to become as you fulfill the full measure of your creation.

A PECULIAR PEOPLE

Excerpted from the Oracles of Celestine Light: Vivus: Chapter 68

And it came to pass that Yeshua remained among the Communities of Light for one moon and taught both his Apostles and all the Children of Light in the use of herbs and minerals.

2 He explained the properties of 111 herbs and minerals and specifically how to use them with prudence for the healing of the body, to make potions, and for many other purposes.

3 Many of the Children of Light were quite surprised to learn that plants and rocks that they walked by every day could be used as such powerful tools of light, when applied with understanding.

4 But amongst the 111 herbs and minerals, which Yeshua taught to them that day, there were many that were rare and not to be found in the land of Galilee.

5 To procure these uncommon plants and minerals, Yeshua charged Gurion of Ptolemais and Gimiel of Capharsalama to journey together to the north and south, and east and west, to obtain the items of which he taught that could not be found in Galilee or even Palestine.

6 They were each given three gold coins and twenty

of silver from the treasury of the communities to fulfill their callings and set out to do as Yeshua bid once he was finished with his teaching to the Children of Light. (Though they returned from time to time to the Communities of Light, ten moons passed before they had procured all that Yeshua had asked them to find.)

7 Yeshua further instructed the Children of Light, concerning their dress and adornment, saying, "You have heard me say that it does not matter to Elohim how you choose to dress or adorn yourself or grow or cut your hair, save you do so with cleanliness and dignity, as is fitting of a temple of Elohim that you are.

8 But you have also heard me say that it is both the inside and the outside of the cup that matters and not just one or the other. And though your choice of adornment is of no consequence to Elohim, it is of greater consequence to you than you have imagined.

9 In the world, there are people who think that only the outside is important. They imagine that rich clothes make them like kings or that a beardless face shows that they are still young.

10 Then there are those who do not care for the outside, and they often look and smell like a dung heap. They think only the deeper inner things of the spirit are important, so they disdain taking time to maintain the outside in cleanliness or beauty.

11 But I say unto you unequivocally that a path that looks only at the outside or only at the inside is a path of little understanding in the Celestine Light. Verily, it is only a path that strives for the purity and cleanliness of both the inside and the outside that finds the greatest

light.

12 Therefore, take care to not be enticed by either a greater love for the inside or the outside, but to maintain both in a harmonious balance, for together they are your temple.

13 When looking to the inside, see that you do not become overly pious. Do not think that in your devotions you are above another, but judge none and seek only to improve yourself. Others will emulate your example if they find it worthy.

14 But when looking to the things of the outside, there are many more traps of which you must beware, for more than the inside, the outside calls to your vanities and entices you into the ways of the world.

15 Not long ago, it was the fashion for both men and women to grease their hair and body with perfumed oil. Those who followed this fashion proclaimed the joy of covering the stink of their unwashed body by a perfume that attested to their personality and with heavy oil that gave them a gloss of sensuality and the slipperiness of a wet frog.

16 And true enough, some women of Palestine would pass by veiled and covered from head to foot but of who it was that passed there was no doubt, for the heaviness of their distinctive perfume proclaimed them.

17 The people of the world are like a flock of sheep who blindly follow the leader wherever they go. Therefore, when one who is admired or of elevated rank in society begins to apply perfumes and gloss themselves with oil, the rest of the sheep think that they must emulate this fashion that they too may be considered in a similar

light of admiration.

18 What of you, Children of Light? You are a divine priesthood, a peculiar people, a chosen generation, for you have a fullness of the Celestine Light of Elohim. Are you in the world but not of it, or have you followed after the fashions and styles of the world?

19 Lest anyone is tempted to dress and adorn themselves in the ways of the world, let them ask themselves this question: Who am I trying to impress?

20 For to dress and adorn as the world dresses and adorns in the passing moment of current fashion can only be meant to impress people of the world, as this has not been asked of you by Elohim.

21 Then how is it that you can impress Elohim in the way that you dress and adorn yourself? Simply by honoring the creation and magnifying it.

22 Consider that Elohim has already dressed and adorned you with the color of your skin, eyes, and hair, and the shape of your face and body.

23 For most men, you have been given that as you mature, hair begins to grow on your face and for both men and women that the hair on your head does not cease to grow at any age, but does turn silver for many as the years pass.

24 Therefore, consider that, for both men and women, your hair is one of the greatest adornments given to you by Elohim and a true reflection of your outward beauty if you care for that which you have been given.

25 Does that mean that every man and woman should just let their hair grow unabated and unattended? Nay, it does not. To show love and honor for the outside of

your temple, you must keep it clean and be creative with styles and adornment of both your hair and your beard, in ways of respect, even as a gardener weeds his garden and arranges it to best showcase the beauty of the flowers and herbs.

26 Some of you have adopted the styles of the Romans and Greeks wherein men remove the hair from their face, with the pain of such action to ever remind them that they are taking away that which Elohim has given.

27 Likewise, some cut the hair of their head very short, even to the point of bareness such as with slaves, for thus do some of the Romans, and it is the fashion, is it not?

28 And the fashion today among Roman and Greek women is to remove all hair from the face and body except a shoulder crop on the head and then to draw on fake eyebrows to replace the real ones that were ripped out. Even many men are emulating this torturous style that requires plucking, burning, and caustic herbs.

29 I am not here to reproach you. In truth, it is important for you to be pleased with your own appearance, and what you choose to do with your body hair is of little consequence to me or our Mother and Father in Heaven.

30 Keep it or remove it as it makes you happy, as its main purpose is to alert you when bugs alight on your skin and to hold your scent. But the hair of your head and beard is another matter.

31 If you remove your beard or cut off the hair of your head or if a woman shortens her hair substantially so it no longer falls at least below the blades of her shoulders,

consider why you are making that choice and if in doing so you are showing the greatest honor to your creator and to the most glorious temple you have been given.

32 If you are not doing it because it is the current fashion and are not doing it out of disrespect to Elohim, who created you and gave you hair that desires to grow long, but only because that choice of appearance makes you most humbly proud of who you are as a son or daughter of God, then Elohim will not look upon you with disfavor and neither should anyone else.

33 I just ask for you to consider thoughtfully and prayerfully how you choose to create your appearance and how you adorn your body, and in this, I would give you some thoughts to ponder upon.

34 Let us first consider the hair of your head. If never cut, for many it would be down below their waist and even to their knees before they died. So there is practicality in trimming it from time to time. But how much is a goodly amount and how much is excessive to the point that perhaps you are dishonoring Elohim the creator or injuring yourself in ways that you are unaware?

35 I tell you with words of soberness that there is far more to this than the honoring of the creator.

36 Remember the story of mighty Samson and how it was his hair that gave him strength? The Roman men cut their hair very short, and they think it makes them more fearsome and less like women who tend to have longer hair, but verily, I say unto you it is the opposite of what they suppose.

37 Your hair is your crown; even for those men who

may lose some of their hair as they age. Elohim would not have created you with endlessly growing hair unless there was a very important reason for it. And that reason is that your hair is a special reservoir of your Celestine power and mystical gifts as Children of Light.

38 It is for this cause that women, more than men, more often exhibit the special gifts of the Children of Light, for it is they who tend to allow their hair to grow long and by that hold much power unto them, waiting to be called upon in time of need.

39 Though men and women, who are Children of Light, may be of equal faith and love, the women will more often be able to manifest their mystical gifts because their long unblemished hair helps them to call upon their greatest potential and succeed where men fail.

40 Of this, you have a great testimony in my wife Miriam. Many of you have witnessed, and others have heard of her great feats utilizing the sacred power of Celestine Light. Many assume it is because she has been so long with me, and there is truth in this. But no less is it because like Samson, she has never cut her hair, save to trim the ends. Nor has she ever poisoned it with caustic dyes or dyes of incongruent color or with suffocating or perfumed oils. And like Samson, her lustrous hair is a reservoir of power that has served her well.

41 Nevertheless, it is among men, few though they are, that more often the greatest power in the gifts of the Children of Light can be seen, for they have the advantage of being able to grow hair not only from their head, but also from their face, perhaps a compensation

for the hair they often lose on their head as they age.

42 Let us now consider the coverings of poison that have been in fashion to put upon the hair. Of what use is a torch if it is covered? And of what use is a reservoir of power, even long hair, if it is suffocated beneath a heavy perfumed oil or altered from its natural color with an indigo or henna dye, changing it from the perfect form and color Elohim created just for you to maximize your ability to harmonize with your essence and call up the power of Celestine Light?

43 Yet in the world both men and women cut their hair. Men remove the hair from their face; both use dyes to change their natural color or cover their hairs of silver and heavy oils to gloss them. Why? All this in the pursuit of false youthfulness that is more truly realized by good food and a brisk and physical life.

44 And why does a man or woman that is married, as all are at a youthful age, have the need to look younger than they are? Will their husband or wife love them any less because they look their age? Are they afraid that their mate will look for someone younger if they do not look younger themselves? Or are they playing with fire and with adulterous thoughts trying to catch the attention of someone who is not their husband or wife?

45 Even as Elohim created man and woman with hair that always grows, so too were they made that in their latter years for many, their hair may become tinged with silver and even all white. Again, other than from a vain desire to appear younger than their true years, why would a man or woman seek to counter that which Elohim has given to mark the span of years and maintain

a harmony with your knowledge and experiences?

46 Please understand clearly that retaining your natural hair color at every age supports the harmony of your essence and facilitates the calling forth of your Celestine powers.

47 Only when your hair color results from disease or poor health is this not true. Then it is another issue that must be first addressed, not with dyes, but with healing and wholeness.

48 In truth, most people who become silver-haired do so years prematurely because of their incorrect diet. Instead of eating foods filled with life, they eat foods full of death. Because of this, their hair turns silver before its time, and they die many years before their time.

49 If without vanity and with harmony, you simply do not desire silver hair, then eat the herbs and foods I have told you, and for most, your hair will retain its natural color until the day you die and return to its former glory if the silver has already appeared.

50 But for some, even with all this, silver hair will still arrive. If it does, realize it offers you greater power if you embrace it because it is has been given to you by Elohim to most purely harmonize with your essence.

51 If your diet does not maintain the color of your hair of youth and for your self-esteem you still cringe to see the silver, then cover it only with gentle natural herbs and only in your natural color; else, you create a significant disharmony in your aura that cannot be overcome in ways other than returning your hair to its natural color.

52 "I have spoken at length about hair, which to

many would seem a trivial subject, inconsequential to spirituality. But among you, the Children of Light, I hope you now understand that the condition of the hair of your head is of great consequence, for it is one of your most important reservoirs of power and you will never be able to become master Adepts of all the secrets of Celestine Light that could be yours if you cut and treat your hair and beards as poorly as do the people of the world.

53 How is it that hair is such a reservoir? Verily, it is the record keeper of the aeon of every experience of your life. Your hair grows about the width of a fingernail each moon, more if it is very healthy from a good diet and not being attacked with heavy oils and caustic dyes.

54 That fingernail of growth has aurically stored all of the experiences, both good and bad, that you have had during that moon. Those experiences remain an energy within you, no less powerful than when you experienced them.

55 Your mind may remember the events, but your hair remembers the energy, if it has not been poisoned by heavy perfumed oils or caustic or incongruent dyes.

56 Whether your experiences were good or bad is irrelevant once you understand the secrets of how to use the aeon stored in your hair and harness it to help empower your special gifts.

57 Even anger has a beneficial power if it is righteous, and even that which hurt you in the past can be called upon and aided by the energy stored in your hair, to help you in the present.

58 There are several things which contribute to your

ability to use your gifts. Chief among these are faith and love, but also important are knowledge, courage, self-confidence, tools that magnify and focus, and a reservoir of power in your temple to call upon. A wise Child of Light will seek after all of these things.

59 Now I would also speak to you somewhat about your adornment and dress. Be not gaudy such as harlots of the world, but neither absent of adornment such as the zealots.

60 Would you build a temple to Elohim out of stone and then put no further adornments upon it to beautify it and make it special and unique? No, instead you would build it of the finest stone and then enhance its appearance with gold and gems and fine woods and carvings placed with elegance and dignity.

61 All throughout the temple you built to Elohim, you would inscribe the sacred symbols of power, unknown to the world but given to the Children of Light.

62 As you would do this for a temple of stone built to Elohim, should you do any less with the temple that you are, which Elohim has created for your glory and exaltation? In no way should you appear like the people of the world in your clothing and adornment. I tell you plainly that you should not look like them. Again, I speak not of gaudiness or extravagance or garishness, but of color, quality, uniqueness, and style.

63 Adorn yourselves not with copper or silver, for their usefulness in calling the Celestine Light is not so great, but only with gold, even if it is only threads woven into your garments, for this is the metal through which the powers of the Celestine Light easily flow.

64 In the stones that you choose to wear in your rings and pendants and other adornments, abandon the glass trinkets of the world and choose only those stones of power which I have taught you, that you may always have near-at-hand tools to aid you in the use of your special gifts of the Celestine Light.

65 If you fashion jewelry of gold, let it contain some of the secret symbols of power. Others may be intrigued by them, but only a true Child of Light steeped in knowledge will know their meaning and how to use them.

66 In your clothing, please do not wear drab colors like the people of the world, for the colors of their clothes are a reflection of their conformity to the fashion of the day or to the poor state of their spirit.

67 Rather, choose to wear bright and cheerful colors, even if only accents upon a predominance of white, that you will draw to you aeons of the same. In this, be not gaudy, for you are not court entertainers, but in all things show the class of Celestines, for more noble than kings and queens you are."

68 Then Yeshua began to teach the Children of Light many of the secrets of which he had spoken that they knew not, including further enlightenment upon sacred symbols, and how to use tools of focus and gold and gemstones and the formulas for many healing elixirs and potions of power.

69 These things cannot be written, but only spoken of in secret among the Children of Light, for Yeshua commanded those of the light not to cast their pearls before swine or reveal the sacred mysteries of Elohim

to the world, which could comprehend their divine purposes not at all.

70 As he has spoken, so shall it forever be.

SERMON OF PARABLES

Excerpted from the Oracles of Celestine Light: Vivus: Chapter 84

Parable of the Sower

That same day, Yeshua stood outside the temple and preached in parables to the large crowd that had come to see him.

161 And he said unto them, "A farmer went out to sow his seed. As he was scattering the seed, some fell along the path, and the birds came and ate it up.

162 Some fell on rocky places, where it did not have much soil. It sprang up quickly, because the soil was shallow. But when the sun came up, the plants were scorched, and they withered because they had no root.

163 Other seed fell among thorns, which grew up and choked the plants. Still other seed fell on good soil, where it produced a crop—a hundred, sixty, or thirty times what was sown. He who has ears, let him hear."

Parable of the Weeds

164 Yeshua told them another parable, saying, "The Kingdom of Heaven is like a man who sowed good seed in his field. But while everyone was sleeping, his enemy came and sowed weeds among the wheat and went away. When the wheat sprouted and formed heads, then the weeds also appeared.

165 The owner's servants came to him and said, 'Sir, didn't you sow good seed in your field? Where then did the weeds come from?'

166 "An enemy did this,' he replied.

167 The servants asked him, 'Do you want us to go and pull them up?'

168 'No,' he answered, 'because while you are pulling the weeds, you may uproot the wheat with them. Let both grow together until the harvest. At that time, I will tell the harvesters: First collect the weeds and tie them in bundles to be burned, then gather the wheat and bring it into my barn.'"

Parable of the Tiny Unknown Seed

169 Then he told them another parable: "The Kingdom of Heaven is like a small unknown seed, which a man took and planted in his field because it appeared unique and curious.

170 Though it was tiny, when it grew, it became a tree, so vast that the birds of the air came and perched in its branches and built nests and thrived."

Parable of the Yeast

171 He told them still another parable: "The Kingdom of Heaven is also like yeast that a woman took and mixed into a large amount of flour until it worked all through the dough."

172 Yeshua spoke all these things to the crowd in parables, and he did not say anything to them without using a parable.

173 So it was fulfilled that which was spoken through

the prophet: "I will open my mouth in parables. I will utter things hidden since the creation of the world."

174 For a moment, Yeshua stopped speaking and told the multitude to remain while he rested a moment. Then the Apostles came to him and asked, "Why do you speak to the people in parables?"

175 Yeshua replied, "The knowledge of the secrets of the Kingdom of Heaven have been given to you, but not to them, because you have seen the light and embraced it into your heart, but they have seen the light yet kept their hearts closed.

176 Whoever has been a good steward of his life will be given more, and he will have an abundance. Whoever has not been a good steward, even what he has will be taken from him.

177 This is why I speak to them in parables. Though seeing, they do not see; though hearing, they do not hear or understand. In them is fulfilled the prophecy of Isaiah: 'You will be ever hearing but never understanding; you will be ever seeing but never perceiving.

178 For the hearts of these people have become calloused; they hardly hear with their ears, and they have closed their eyes.'

179 Otherwise, they might see with their eyes, hear with their ears, understand with their hearts, and turn to the Celestine Light, and then I would heal more than the infirmities of their body. I would enliven their spirit with the light that is never extinguished.

180 But blessed are your eyes because they see and your ears because they hear. Many prophets and righteous men longed to see what you have seen, but

did not see it, and to hear what you have heard, but did not hear it.

181 Listen now to what the parable of the sower means: When anyone hears the message about the Kingdom and does not understand it, the adversary within comes and snatches away what was sown in his heart. This is the seed sown along the path.

182 The one who received the seed that fell on rocky places is the man who hears the word and at once receives it with joy. But since he has no root, he lasts only a short time. When trouble or persecution comes because of the word, the adversary within steals his courage, and he quickly falls away.

183 The one who received the seed that fell among the thorns is the man who hears the word, but the adversary within allows the worries of this life and the deceitfulness of wealth to choke it, making it unfruitful.

184 But the one who received the seed that fell on good soil is the man who hears the word and understands it. He overcomes the adversary within and produces a crop, yielding a hundred, sixty, or thirty times what was sown."

185 "Can you also explain the parable of the weeds?" asked Salome.

186 Yeshua nodded in affirmation and said unto them, "The one who sowed the good seed is the Son of Light.

187 The field is the world, and the good seed stands for the sons and daughters of the Kingdom.

188 The weeds are the people of the world who sin without repentance and restitution and the enemy who sows them is Lucifer, who ever works to bring out the

worst in all people and stir the adversary within.

189 The harvest is the end of the mortal life, and the harvesters are angels.

190 As the weeds are pulled up and burned in the fire, so it will be at the end of the mortal life of they who acquiesced to the adversary within and sowed darkness instead of light.

191 The Son of Light shall send out his angels, and they will weed out his Kingdom of everything that invites and entices to sin, and all the weak of will who have given into the adversary within and given excuse to evil rather than sincere repentance and restitution.

192 The wages of unrepentant sin are torment of the soul, because those of darkness cannot bear the brightness of the light, but they shall still long forlornly for the light they cannot bear.

193 The angels will release them to be drawn by their own resonance into the fiery furnace, fueled by their own despair for what might have been. There they shall remain, wallowing in the torment of their own creation, within the darkness they can scarcely bear, until they become greater than their adversary within and return to the glory of the light through repentance and restitution.

194 The wheat are the righteous, those that have endeavored continually to do good and sincerely and fully repented when they have done wrong, and they will shine like the sun with me in the Kingdom of Heaven, forever."

Parable of the Hidden Treasure

195 Then Yeshua spoke again to the multitude in parables, saying, "The Kingdom of Heaven is like a treasure hidden in a field. When a man found it, in his joy, he went and sold all he had and bought that field."

Parable of the Pearl of Great Value

196 "Again, the Kingdom of Heaven is like a merchant looking for fine pearls. When he found one of great value, he went away and sold everything he had and bought it, for its worth exceeded all else."

Parable of the Fish in the Net

197 "Once again, the Kingdom of Heaven is like a net that was let down into the lake and caught all kinds of fish. When it was full, the fishermen pulled it up on the shore. Then they sat down and collected the good fish in baskets, but threw the bad away."

198 This is how it will be at the end of mortality. The angels will come and separate the wicked from the righteous and release the wicked to be drawn into the fiery furnace by their disharmonious resonance. And there shall be much weeping and wailing and gnashing of teeth.

199 In the world of the darkness and fire, the wicked will see what could have so easily been in the world of the light. But even seeing, even knowing and understanding how simple it would be to change, most will still be unwilling to walk the path of repentance and turn torment into joy because of the restitution they would have to make.

200 Have you understood all these things?" Yeshua

asked. "Yes," they replied.

201 May your affirmation lead you to greater light," Yeshua encouraged. "Therefore, every teacher of the law who has been instructed about the true Celestine Light of the Kingdom of Heaven is like the owner of a house, who brings out of his storeroom new treasures, as well as old."

Unwashed Hands

202 Then some Pharisees and teachers of the law came to Yeshua and asked, "Why do your Apostles break the tradition of the elders? They don't wash their hands before they eat!"

203 Yeshua replied with a laugh, "Can you not think of something new to ask? Only when you are near do they not wash their hands, for I have asked them not to do so whenever they see you, to refute your traditions.

204 A greater question is why do you break the command of Elohim for the sake of your tradition? For in the commandments of Sinai, Elohim said, 'Honor your father and mother.' But you say that it is acceptable if a man says to his father or mother, 'Whatever help you might otherwise have received from me, I cannot give, for it is a gift devoted to God.'

205 Thus you nullify the word of God for the sake of your tradition. You hypocrites! Isaiah was right when he prophesied about you: 'These people honor me with their lips, but their hearts are far from me. They worship me in vain, and their teachings are but rules taught by men.'"

206 Yeshua called the crowd to him and said, "Listen

and understand. What goes into a man's mouth does not make him unclean, unhealthy perhaps, but not unclean. But what comes out of his mouth; that is what makes him unclean before Elohim."

207 Then the Apostles came to him, and Cephas said, "You are making more enemies every day. You know that the Pharisees were greatly offended when they heard what you said?"

208 Yeshua answered him, saying, "Every plant that does not grow under the light of our Heavenly Mother and Father will be pulled up by the roots.

209 Do not concern yourselves with them or those who follow them; they are blind guides. If a blind man leads a blind man, both will fall into a pit."

210 Yohhanan then asked, "Will you also explain the last parable to us."

211 Yeshua replied, "Lest I begin to think you are dull or not listening closely yourself, why don't you tell us what it means, for I will not long be with you to answer such questions."

212 Yohhanan stammered a little as he was put on the spot and tried to answer, but then he found his voice and replied, "Whatever enters the mouth goes into the stomach and then out of the body. So though it may be unhealthy and make a man sick if he does not eat with prudence, it is not unclean.

213 "But the things that come out of the mouth, the words a man speaks, these come from his heart, and these are the things that make a man unclean if they are contrary to the Celestine Light of Elohim.

214 For out of the heart can come evil thoughts,

murder, adultery, sexual immorality, theft, false testimony, slander, and many more things of darkness.

215 Certainly, these are what make a man unclean, but eating with unwashed hands, though not wise, does not make him unclean."

216 "Well spoken!" Yeshua exclaimed. "Now all of you, remember to ponder upon my words often that you may understand them fully. Be at peace in your heart and in love with the light, and surely the Holy Spirit of Elohim will ever enlighten you to the greater truths."

Parable of the Two Sons

217 Turning again to the multitude that had gathered to hear him speak, Yeshua noticed that more Sadducees and Pharisees had appeared among the crowd near him.

218 And he spoke to them again in parables, saying, "What do you think? There was a man who had two sons. He went to the first and said, 'Son, go and work today in the vineyard.'

219 'I will not,' he answered, but later he changed his mind and went.

220 Then the father went to the other son and said the same thing. He answered, 'I will, sir,' but he did not go."

221 Addressing the Sadducees and Pharisees directly, Yeshua asked, "Which of the two did what his father wanted?"

222 "The first," they answered. And Yeshua replied to them, "And you are like unto the second. Verily, the tax collectors and the prostitutes will enter the Kingdom of Heaven ahead of you, for they have seen the error of their ways and have been humbled unto repentance.

But you, seeing the error of your sins, remain haughty and full of words that justify, but empty of deeds that testify.

223 Remember my brother Yochanan? He came to you to show you the way of righteousness, and you did not believe him, but the tax collectors and the prostitutes did. And even after you saw this and heard the purity of the light as it was spoken from his lips, you did not repent and believe him. What is this sand you stand upon?

Parable of the Unworthy Tenants

224 "Listen to another parable: There was a landowner who planted a vineyard. He put a wall around it, dug a winepress in it, and built a watchtower. Then he rented the vineyard to some farmers and went away on a journey.

225 When the harvest time approached, he sent his servants to the tenants to collect his fruit.

226 The tenants seized his servants; they beat one, killed another, and stoned a third.

227 Then he sent other servants to them, more than the first time, and the tenants treated them the same way.

228 Last of all, he sent his son to them. They will respect my son, he thought.

229 But when the tenants saw the son, they said to each other, 'This is the heir. Come, let's kill him and take his inheritance.'

230 So they took him and threw him out of the vineyard and killed him.

231 Therefore, when the owner of the vineyard comes, what will he do to those tenants?"

232 He will bring those wretches to a wretched end," they replied, "And he will rent the vineyard to other tenants, who will give him his share of the crop at harvest time."

233 Yeshua said to them, "Have you never read in the scriptures: 'The stone the builders rejected has become the capstone; the Lord has done this, and it is marvelous in our eyes?'

234 Therefore, I tell you that like the evil tenants, you have failed in your stewardship, and the Kingdom of God will be taken away from you and given to a people who will produce its fruit.

235 Like Belshazzar, you have been weighed in the balance and found wanting, and your Kingdom shall be given to another. He who falls on this stone will be broken to pieces, and he on whom it falls will be crushed."

236 When the chief priests and the Pharisees heard the parables of Yeshua, they were greatly offended, for it was obvious to everyone that in many of his stories, he was talking about them. They looked then for a way to arrest him, but they were afraid of the crowd because the people held that he was a prophet and a healer sent by God.

Parable of the Wedding Banquet

237 Yeshua spoke to the religious leaders and the multitude again in parables, saying: "The Kingdom of Heaven is like a king who prepared a wedding banquet for his son.

238 He sent his servants to those who had been invited to the banquet to tell them to come, but they refused to come.

239 Then he sent some more servants and said, 'Tell those who have been invited that I have prepared my dinner, every type of delicacy imaginable, and everything is ready. Come to the wedding banquet.'

240 But the invitees paid no attention and went off—one to his field, another to his business. The rest seized his servants, mistreated them, and killed some of them. The king was enraged. He sent his army and destroyed those murderers and burned their city.

241 Then he said to his servants, 'The wedding banquet is ready, but those I invited did not deserve to come. Go to the street corners and invite to the banquet anyone you find. But tell them to come prepared for the occasion and to give the honor that is due.'

242 So the servants went out into the streets and gathered all the people they could find, both the good and bad who said they would come prepared and willing to give the honor that was due, and the wedding hall was filled with guests.

243 But when the king came in to see the guests, he noticed a man there who was not wearing wedding clothes. 'Friend,' he said, 'You disrespect me and the honor I have given you. Why are you here without wedding clothes?' The man was speechless to have been caught unprepared, for he had thought to partake of the banquet without needing to pay tribute to the king.

244 Then the king told the attendants, 'Tie him hand and foot, and throw him outside, into the darkness,

where there will be weeping and wailing and gnashing of teeth for what has been lost and could have been.'

245 Verily, many are invited to partake of the Celestine Light, but few are worthy to be chosen."

Parable of the Ten Virgins

246 And he spoke another parable unto them, saying, "The Kingdom of Heaven will be like ten virgins who took their lamps and went out to meet the bridegroom.

247 Five of them were foolish, and five were wise. The foolish ones took their lamps but did not take any oil with them. The wise, however, took oil in jars along with their lamps. The bridegroom was a long time in coming, and they all became drowsy and fell asleep.

248 At midnight, the cry rang out: 'Here's the bridegroom! Come out to meet him!'

249 Then all the virgins woke up and trimmed their lamps. The foolish ones said to the wise, 'Give us some of your oil; our lamps are going out.'

250 'No,' they replied, 'we have prepared ourselves to be ready for the bridegroom, and we do not have enough oil for both us and you. You must go instead to those who sell oil and buy some for yourselves.'

251 But while they were on their way to buy the oil, the bridegroom arrived. The virgins who were ready went in with him to the wedding banquet. And the door was shut.

252 Later the others also came. 'Sir! Sir!' they said. 'Open the door for us!'

253 But he replied, 'Your lamps were needed at the beginning, and now there is no place for you.'

254 Therefore, be prepared. Live your life each day in ways that are worthy of the Celestine Light within you and the eternal reward that awaits the valiant because you do not know the day or the hour when your soul shall be called to come before Elohim to be weighed in the balance."

Parable of the Talents Multiplied

255 "Again, I urge you not to neglect the stewardship of your life. It is like a man going on a journey who called his servants and entrusted his property to them. To one, he gave five talents of money, to another two talents, and to another one talent, each according to his ability. Then he went on his journey.

256 The man who had received the five talents went at once and put his money to work and gained five more. So also, the one with the two talents gained two more. But the man who had received the one talent went off, dug a hole in the ground, and hid his master's money.

257 After a long time, the master of those servants returned and settled accounts with them. The man who had received the five talents brought the other five. 'Master,' he said, 'you entrusted me with five talents. See, I have gained five more.'

258 His master replied, 'Well done, good and faithful servant! You have been faithful with a few things; I will put you in charge of many things. Come and share your master's happiness!'

259 The man with the two talents also came. 'Master,' he said, 'you entrusted me with two talents. See, I have gained two more.'

260 His master replied, 'Well done, good and faithful servant! You have been faithful with a few things; I will put you in charge of many things. Come and share your master's happiness!'

261 Then the man who had received the one talent came. 'Master,' he said, 'I knew that you are a hard man, harvesting where you have not sown and gathering where you have not scattered seed. So I was afraid and went out and hid your talent in the ground. See, here is what belongs to you.'

262 His master replied, 'You wicked, lazy servant! So you knew that I harvest where I have not sown and gather where I have not scattered seed? Well then, you should have put my money on deposit with the bankers so that when I returned, I would have at least received it back with some interest.'

263 'Take the talent from him and give it to the one who has the ten talents,' he ordered.

264 'For everyone who multiplies will be given more, and he will have an abundance. But whoever does not multiply, even what he has will be taken from him.

265 'And throw that worthless servant outside, into the darkness, where there will be weeping and wailing and gnashing of teeth for what might have been.'"

Parable of Helping a Stranger

266 "When the Son of Light reigns in his majesty, and all the angels with him, he will sit on his throne in heavenly glory. All the nations will be gathered before him, and he will separate the people one from another as a shepherd separates the sheep from the goats. He

will put the sheep on his right and the goats on his left.

267 Then the king will say to those on his right, 'Come, you who are blessed by my Father and Mother; take your inheritance, the Kingdom prepared for you since the creation of the world.

268 'For I was hungry, and you gave me something to eat; I was thirsty, and you gave me something to drink; I was a stranger, and you invited me in; I needed clothes, and you clothed me; I was sick, and you looked after me; I was in prison, and you came to visit me.'

269 Then the righteous will answer him, 'Lord, when did we see you hungry and feed you or thirsty and give you something to drink? When did we see you a stranger and invite you in; or needing clothes and clothe you? When did we see you sick or in prison and go to visit you?'

270 The king will reply, 'Verily, whatever you did for one of the least of these brothers or sisters of mine, you did for me.'

271 Then he will say to those on his left, 'Depart from me, you who were selfish, into the tormenting fire prepared for the unworthy. For I was hungry and you gave me nothing to eat, I was thirsty and you gave me nothing to drink, I was a stranger and you did not invite me in, I needed clothes and you did not clothe me, I was sick and in prison and you did not look after me.'

272 They also will answer, 'Lord, when did we see you hungry or thirsty or a stranger or needing clothes or sick or in prison and did not help you?'

273 He will reply, 'Verily, whatever you did not do for one of the least of these my brothers and sisters, you did

not do for me.'

274 Then they will go away to the torment they have earned by their selfishness, but the righteous will enter into eternal life and glory because of their selfless love."

275 Then Yeshua was finished speaking, and he departed again to Bethany to be with his children for the evening.

SERMON BY THE JORDON

Excerpted from the Oracles of Celestine Light: Vivus: Chapter 92

And it came to pass that Yeshua remained upon the earth for forty days after his resurrection.

2 The first six days following his return, he went in secret to the house of Lazarus in Bethany with Miriam, Salome, and Martha and spent much time with all of their children.

3 Yeshua instructed the Apostles to also go and be with their families for six days. And so they all did.

Teachings in the Wilderness of Jordan

4 On the morning of the seventh day, Yeshua, Miriam, Salome, and all of the Apostles, including Yudas Iscariot, departed from Bethany and went into the wilderness near the Jordan River, and Yeshua began to teach them more of the mysteries of Celestine Light and the powers given unto them as Apostles and Children of Light.

5 They remained encamped near the Jordan for several days. Each day during the late afternoon Yeshua would answer questions that were asked, and many mysteries were revealed by his answers, most of which cannot be written and recorded, but only spoken of within the Sacred Circles of the Children of Light.

6 The first day together in the wilderness, everyone

was caught up in the excitement of all of the marvels they were learning from Yeshua and they did not want the day to end so much so that they pleaded with him to keep teaching them well into the night by the light of the Moon and stars, and he did as they asked.

7 When he was finished speaking in the late hours of the night, Yeshua departed from them all and promised he would return again in the morning.

8 When the morning arrived, the Apostles were still in the throngs of fatigue. The sun was already rising in the sky when Miriam came to where the men were sleeping to wake them, "Rouse yourselves brothers; you must be alert, for the Lord of Light comes even now."

9 Suddenly there was a bright light upon the ground, and Yeshua stood before them. Miriam came to him, and he held her and kissed her tenderly.

10 Then came Salome, and she fell to her knees and made to kiss his feet, but he raised her up and held her with Miriam and kissed her lightly on the lips.

11 Yeshua spoke to everyone present, saying, "I will not linger long upon the earth, but ere I go for the last time, I shall teach you in the coming days the fullest mysteries of the Kingdom of Heaven and the Celestine Light, which comes from it.

12 You shall learn that which you have never known or imagined. And with the knowledge I give, you will hold some of the power of the Elohim and will be able to do all manner of wonders, as long as you remain humble, and worthy stewards of the Celestine Light you are given.

13 Many of the things I shall reveal to you are the

means to change that which is seen into something that is not seen, to affect and alter the minds of men and matter, to cause the properties of one substance to change into another, and to travel in spirit anywhere in this world and beyond at the speed of thought to witness any event or to discover any secret of men.

14 Some of the things you shall learn can only be accomplished by worthy Children of Light having great experience and understanding of the foundations of Celestine Light that uphold all things which exist.

15 Others can be mastered even by the Ganish, simply by following the steps that open the secret doors to the unseen powers of Celestine Light that uphold the world that the world knows not.

16 Because these are merely steps taken in an exact manner to produce a result, they can be done by anyone who follows the steps, even the unworthy. Therefore, you must guard the secrets of the steps zealously, lest they become known to the unworthy who would call forth the hidden currents of power for unrighteous purposes.

17 Therefore, I give you a sacred trust: keep the secrets of that which I reveal only in your heads. Never let them be recorded upon a scroll that the unworthy could unveil and read.

18 With some secrets I teach, there is power simply in the form to call in the force, and this by anyone that follows the form, both the worthy and the unworthy, the righteous and the unrighteous.

19 And it shall come to pass that a handful of the secrets of the forms shall escape into the world, for

the virtuous do not always remain so, and some shall stumble by the wayside.

20 Then shall there also be times when you will be seen by the Ganish calling upon the powers of Celestine Light and doing things which in the minds of men cannot be done.

21 In their observation there will be a remembrance of the form, even unto the words you said and the substances you mixed and the movements you made.

22 And so shall they emulate. A few will succeed in calling in some of the powers that can be called in by the forms of simplicity, even as priests, witches, and sorcerers have been able to do since the days when they saw the first Children of Light using the powers of Heaven upon the earth.

23 Thus it shall come to pass that some of the forms and a small part of the power shall come to be known and used by witches, sorcerers, and priests seeking to wield a power they know not, some for purposes of good and some for evil.

24 A little healing they will do, but to them, it will seem great. Small miracles they will accomplish, and though feeble, they shall acclaim them from the mountaintops.

25 But worry not at all for this. The true power of Celestine Light, even to say unto a mountain to take up and be cast into the sea, or unto the paralytic to rise up and walk or to the storm to come or go, they will be incapable of accomplishing.

26 Though they may know some of the forms that call in the power, they can never possess the Celestine Light of Elohim that is the activating force behind the greatest

powers.

27 Only a worthy Child of Light can be one in completeness with the Celestine Light. And only by being one with the power of the light can it be called forth in its fullness and majesty.

28 Therefore, always remember: There is far greater effect when the form is wielded by the righteous and virtuous, and greater still when it is manifested by those who are Children of Light that have been set apart and ordained by Elohim to be stewards of the Celestine Light, even as each of you has been, my brothers and sisters.

29 And it is not because of the witches and priests that you must never write the secrets of the inner sanctum, for they too will keep the secrets that they know, but to protect this knowledge from ever being possessed by the Caesars or the foolish.

30 With the Caesars, it is better to rot in prison and even to pass in silence from this life than to reveal that which I shall give to you. For even with a feather of the knowledge of the simplest forms, twisted for evil, they could do great harm upon the land and to the people.

31 Know that you are the stewards, not just of your families and not just of the Family of Light, but of all the earth. It is given to you to protect the land and the great waters upon the vastness and to serve all the inhabitants thereof, both man and beast, even as I have served you.

32 Let your light shine among the children of men that they will open their hearts to the Celestine Light of Elohim that they may become more than they have been, even unto inheriting the glory of the Kingdom to

come.

33 When I have passed beyond this earth, you are ordained to be the bearers of the secrets that I shall give to you.

34 You may share these secrets in fullness only to the worthy who are also baptized Children of Light, who love their bodies as temples inside and out, who have a firm foundation of understanding and proven ability with knowledge already received to warrant new and greater knowledge to be given, who live and cherish the Great Commandment and the Twelve Commandments of Sinai and have been faithful stewards of all that has been given unto them.

Healing the Worthy in Need

35 "You may also use the secret knowledge of Celestines to help any in the world who ask for your help with selflessness and love, in humility, and with sincere repentance of their sins, for all are spirit children of the Father and the Mother and deserving of the blessings of the Celestine Light when they are in harmony with it.

36 As they are prepared to receive the light, so shall it come into them through your hand and a miracle in the eyes of men shall be born.

37 I give you the power to heal both the small and the great, and nothing shall be impossible to you if it is within the will of Elohim to restore the human body to its health and wholeness, if you remain pure and humble and are blessing a Child of Light committed to living as a temple.

38 When those who are not numbered among you seek you out for a blessing, the power of Celestine Light

will flow through you in balance and equality to their faith, purity of heart, repentance of sins, and love for their temple and their fellow brothers and sisters of Elohim upon the earth.

39 Those who have not faith to believe in things unseen and unknown or who are not pure in heart but think selfishly and deviously, or who have not repented of their sins or love not their bodies but destroy their temple with the things they put inside or outside, or care not for the lives of their fellow brothers and sisters of the spirit children of Elohim upon the earth—these have no promise, and they cannot benefit from a blessing.

40 Not because you do not have the power, but because healing is a circle of light. It is only when the circle completes that the healing occurs.

41 You call in the great power of Celestine Light and send it unto those to be healed. In a Child of Light, it is received; it heals, and it is sent back out to you with love and gratitude.

42 But a person of the world cannot send back the light, because they do not really believe in it.

43 They cannot send back the light because their character is flawed, and they do not seek to make the effort to live upon the mountain of higher ideals given to man, but seek instead the easy way, wallowing in the swamp of that which is nothing.

44 They cannot send back the light because they have not repented of their sins, and when the healing light encounters unrepented sins it fades away, for the Celestine Light knows where it is not wanted.

45 They cannot send back the light because they do

not treat their bodies as temples inside and out, and the light will not dwell in polluted waters.

46 They cannot send back the light because they are selfish and make no effort to serve and help their fellow brothers and sisters upon the earth.

47 You are merely the riverbed of the stream that is the Celestine Light of Elohim. The light rushes forth to heal the pure and the less pure and the impure.

48 As each person is open to the Celestine Light and have lived it in their lives, so each shall receive the portion that they can hold—the pure of heart and life made whole, and the less pure made less whole, and the impure not changed.

49 Ponder upon my words for in them are life eternal and dominion over disease and death before its time.

How to Be One with the Elohim

50 "When you are alone, you are a single lamp of the Celestine Light of Elohim, but far from alone, for Elohim—the Father, the Mother, and the Son—are with you. You will forever have their Holy Spirit to guide and direct your paths as long as you live the light.

51 When you are in solitude, call upon the Father and the Mother in my name with focused thought, a clear intent, and a heart that reaches beyond the world, and you will be one with the Elohim, with the Celestine Light, to accomplish the purposes you seek.

52 When you are gathered together, two or more reaching out to the Elohim, you must be of one heart and mind as you call upon the Celestine Light and the power it brings. Focus your thoughts and let your hearts reach out until they touch the heart of Elohim and you

are one with the light."

53 Toma asked, "Great Lord of Light, how may we do this wonder that you describe? How do we focus our thoughts and reach our heart beyond the world until it is one with Elohim and the light?"

54 Yeshua answered, saying, "You are in the world, but you should not be like it. If a man lives in the ways of the world, how would he know how to be one with God?

55 But it has been given to you to know the ways of the Elohim. You hold in your hearts and live in your lives the Great Commandment and the Twelve Commandments of Sinai.

56 You honor and respect your bodies as temples made by the Elohim and eat, sleep, and work in ways that enhance the vitality of your temple.

57 You are continuously on a quest to gain more knowledge of the ways of the Celestine Light, and as your knowledge grows so you are prepared to speak with intelligence to the Elohim about the mysteries of the Kingdom.

58 As you live the way the Elohim live, your spirit is able to pass through the gate of Celestine Light and be in their presence, even as you are worthy vessels to have the Holy Spirit of Elohim upon you that they can come and be in your presence.

59 By this, the table has been set and the meal prepared, and now the Elohim will come and sup at your table.

60 In humble prayer, invite them to come to you and be one with you, and the Holy Spirit will fill your heart and speak in your mind, and you will for a moment transcend the bonds of earth and be one with the

Celestine Light of Elohim in fullness.

61 Herein is the true power that is greater than the form. This is the power of the snake of Moses to eat the snakes of the priests of pharaoh.

62 This is the power that the sons and daughters of Light used to lift the stones of the great pyramids of Egypt for the pharaohs, allowing their community to live in peace and prosperity in the land of the Egyptians and not in subjugation as were the Hebrews and other peoples.

63 This is the power that even if they knew, a witch, a sorcerer, a priest, or a Caesar could never use, for they are unworthy vessels, and the Celestine Light of Elohim cannot dwell within them, nor the fullness of its power."

Cephas Reminisces

64 Then Cephas, who had been sitting, stood up saying, "Good Yeshua, what a marvel this is that each day we still have so much to learn from you!

65 What a wonderful journey you have taken us on! I recall when you used to come to the lake when you were still a young man, and it is overwhelming to remember all that has happened in our lives since then, all we have learned, all we have seen, and the promise of all that is to come.

66 Now you have shared still greater knowledge with us, when already I thought my cup was full and overflowing.

67 I myself am so different now than those long-ago days at the lake that it sometimes seems as if I am visitor from another land as I pass through this place I have

lived near all of my life.

68 I know what the Savasi must have felt like when they first returned to this world and began to live among the people of the land: in some ways just like them, but in others so very different.

69 Forgive me if I ramble. The understanding of the enormity of everything that you are and everything we are because of you has just now come upon me like the eyes of a traveler being opened onto the most amazing vista.

70 I think for the first time, I have truly comprehended all that has transpired in our lives and all that is yet to be." And tears began to well up in his eyes.

71 But he continued speaking through his tears, saying, "Thank you for the honor of being called an Apostle of your light. Thank you for being my guide upon this journey and finding and bringing out the Child of Light that was inside of me; that the gruff fisherman that was on the outside never would have recognized if it were not for you.

72 I am overwhelmed and humbled to the depths of my soul." Then he could speak no more through his tears, and he sat down upon a rock and smiled at those around him, laughing a little at his own emotions.

73 Yeshua came over to Cephas and, offering him his hand, pulled him up and embraced him, saying, "You are welcome, good brother. You are welcome. I have always been honored to call you a friend and a brother, and I always will be.

The Workings of a Circle of Light

74 "But this was not what you actually stood up to say, was it?"

75 Cephas shook his head and answered, "No, I had a question about that which you had just taught us, but the spirit of my soul came over me and the words I spoke came out unbidden from the depths of my heart."

76 Then Cephas put a hand on each of Yeshua's shoulders and laughed lightly as he looked at him, saying, "You see, even those words I just said—very flowery they were—nothing at all like how a normal man should speak and certainly not how I used to speak before I was changed by you."

77 Yeshua laughed back good-naturedly, but then said with calm serenity, "It was not me, Cephas, save perhaps as a catalyst. You simply heard and heeded the call of the greater Cephas beckoning you to become the fullness of the man you can be, even as all men and women are called by the inner voice of their soul to become more than they are, not in the ways of the world, but in the ways of the Celestine Light."

78 Cephas nodded his head in agreement and Yeshua asked him to present the question he had begun to ask, and Cephas did, saying, "You spoke of the circle of light necessary to effect a healing, but how is the circle completed when we call upon the Celestine Light to affect things that are not people, such as moving a mountain?"

79 "All things that exist," began Yeshua, "are creations of the Elohim.

80 Unto man, and others like unto man in intelligence

and experience, has been given the opportunity to freely make choices of light or darkness in every aspect of their lives, beginning with their thoughts.

81 This that they might begin to walk the path that leads to the realm of the Elohim, which realm is far greater than the Celestine Realm of which you have learned so much and aspire even now to gain.

82 Understand that even that may be, for some, just a way point in their eternal progression.

83 For the Celestine Realm, though it is grander than your imagination can conceive, is merely a small part of the greater, more-glorious realm of the Elohim that awaits the most faithful.

84 For where you now are, how you now are, even the Father and Mother once were, and where they now are, how they now are, you may someday become as you continue through this life and time untold that follows to be one with the Celestine Light.

85 When you are one with the light, you are no longer of this world, though your feet may still tread upon it.

86 That is why you feel somewhat disconnected from the world already Cephas. Even in the land and among the people you have known all of your life, as I'm sure all of your brethren do as well." Hearing his words the other Apostles all nodded in agreement.

87 Then Yeshua added a caution, saying, "But while you still live upon this world, never become so much in the next that you forget that it has been given to you to be the faithful stewards of the world upon which you live, to guard it and protect it, and all of the creatures and life therein that are in need of your guardianship

and protection.

88 For all of these, all life upon the earth other than man, are pure in the Celestine Light of their creation. They are innocent of sin, save those that have been corrupted by man, but even then the sin is upon the corrupters, not upon the corrupted.

89 Because the land and the sea and the sky and all creatures therein are innocent and pure in the light, when you call upon the Celestine Light to affect them, the circle is immediately completed as the light runs through them, changes them as you have commanded, and returns to you.

90 The light is of Elohim, and so are all things. And save for man who has been given knowledge of good and evil, the Celestine Light sent out shall always return to the sender, for therein lies its resonance and abode."

Why We Have Commandments

91 Then Yeshua posed a question to the Apostles, asking, "Why do you think your place in the next life depends so much upon your faithfulness in this life to the principles and precepts I have taught?

92 Why did the Elohim bother to give man the Twelve Commandments of Sinai or any of the higher precepts? Man is surely of sound-enough mind and reason to have thought of these principles himself as a way to live in harmony with his fellow man and progress in his life.

93 So why did the Elohim command some things and why have many others been taught to you by me with precept and example many times, in multiple ways, but not by commandment?"

94 Yohhanan lifted his hand, signaling he wished to

answer the question, and Yeshua nodded affirmatively for him to proceed. And Yohhanan answered, saying, "When we hear words of wisdom, such as those from the Greek philosophers, we ponder upon them and reason them out in our mind. We only adopt them in our lives if they seem practical and do not require too much effort for the promised reward.

95 But when we hear or see the same principle given by the Father and Mother or shown or taught to us by you, there is something more that occurs after the pondering and reasoning.

96 With the Greek philosophers, we may understand the truth of a teaching and the wisdom of adopting it in our lives. But as it is just the teaching of a man, we are likely only inclined to act upon it if it does not require too much effort, and the reward is quick to come.

97 Then something similar is taught to us by the Elohim in the words of the old prophets or in the things we see you do or hear you teach. Though there is always a promise of benefit in this life for living the teachings, the greater reward is saved for the eternal life to come, in a world we cannot see, and with faith alone must accept to be real and waiting for the valiant.

98 This then is why I think the Elohim have given us the Twelve Commandments and taught us to follow other higher laws of righteousness that we will do so in faith, with faith abiding and growing inside us.

99 Obeying the commandments and following the precepts make us better people—better husbands and fathers and sons. But so would following the teachings of the philosophers.

100 But building faith is something far greater, for you have taught us that faith is a power, like a fire, and by it all things were created and by it come all miracles. By it, we have command of the Celestine Light.

101 By following the good words of wise men, we can become good men ourselves, but by living in fullness the commandments and teachings of the Elohim can we become men of faith, in whom the Elohim can trust and in whom the power of the Celestine Light can come and abide, in this life and the next.

102 As to why some are commandments and others only admonitions—surely all are of equal worth in our lives, but the handful of commandments have weight beyond their numbers when we are weighed in the balance at the Judgment of Resonance as all the admonitions are truly encompassed within the commandments."

103 As Yohhanan finished speaking, Yeshua walked over to him, and placing a hand on either side of his head, he kissed him lightly on the top of his head, saying, "Truly, Yohhanan, the Holy Spirit has come upon you. You are ready now to bring the Celestine Light to the world, for in you it abides and from you it comes forth."

Concerning Paul

104 Yeshua then addressed something completely different, saying, "As I have spoken about before to you, in the days soon to come, a religion shall build up upon the earth from fragments of my teachings, and it shall cover the world in generations to come.

105 But it will to the greatest extent be based upon the

teachings of a Benjamite named Saul. A learned man who shall at first persecute the Children of Light and anyone who follows even a part of my teachings.

106 Then shall come his day of remorse and repentance and thereafter, he shall be known as Paul, and he shall dedicate his life to building a church throughout the lands of the Romans and Greeks based upon the part of my teachings that appeal to him.

107 He will convert many Gentiles to his church after the name the Greeks call me—Iesous. And he shall call himself my Apostle.

108 But Paul will not be an Apostle such as you are, one who has traveled with me day to day and heard and seen the wonders of Heaven.

109 Nor will he be called by me and set apart and ordained to be my Apostle on earth, to speak and act in my name, or given the great secrets of the Celestine Light, which have been given to you.

110 Nor shall you give these things to Paul or ordain him to be an Apostle or teach him the ways of the Adepts, for he will continually be opposed to the fullness of the Celestine Light and therefore never worthy to receive its greatest secrets and powers.

111 Some of his teachings will be from the teachings of old that are in opposition to that which I have taught, and you will have cause to be angry with him and to cast him out from among you.

112 But this I would ask, my brethren. Love him, even as I have loved you. Teach him what he is ready to learn and be not angry with him for that which he is not ready, for every person should be given the light only

as they are capable of receiving it in good stewardship.

113 Though he will teach some things that are false and omit others that are true and important, the portion of my light that he shall bring upon the world will still be great in many ways, one that shall uplift those that follow it and bring them closer to Elohim in a greater measure than they had been before the teachings of Paul came to them.

114 And that which he shall teach, in my Greek name, shall spread across all of the world and touch the lives of many people, causing many to forsake their sins of the past and live their lives closer to the Celestine Light of Elohim.

115 While that which you teach shall only be for the elect, and they shall not long remain upon the earth, save those who shall remain behind as earth stewards.

116 Verily, the people of the world are not yet ready for the immensity of the Celestine Light you shall bring, and they will be blinded by its brightness until the generation of promise comes forth."

117 "What shall we do with this Paul when he comes?" asked Cephas. "Shall we invite him into our communities? And how shall we teach him all that he should know if he is going to preach even a small part of the Celestine Light you have given us and yet will be opposed to some of the foundations of our understanding?"

118 Yeshua smiled and answered, saying, "You will be like two hawks fighting whenever in each other's presence, unless you both remember to love one another even as I have loved you.

119 Do not condemn him for his weaknesses or the fallacy of his doctrines. Do not find reasons to be angry with him.

120 Correct him as you can with gentleness; help him see as much of the Celestine Light as he can receive by your teachings and the examples of your lives.

121 See the good in him; see the light; see his devotion to service and his eloquent uplifting of his fellow men.

122 When he has received all the Celestine Light from you that he will accept, send him to the Gentiles where he will find fertile ground.

123 Then when you see the children of Paul in churches, springing up across the land, wearing my Greek masquerade of a name; be not offended by them, for they are humble, sincere seekers of the light, even as you are.

124 In truth, Paul will be doing you a favor by bringing his followers closer to the Celestine Light than they previously were and more receptive to the resonance of the greater light that you can bring to those who are ready to receive it.

125 Because of the light Paul first brings, some who become children of Paul shall later become Children of the true Celestine Light and receive it in fullness and be numbered among you."

Finding the Children of Light

126 Another day, Yeshua spoke to Miriam, Salome, and the Apostles further, saying, "You will face many adversities in the days to come. So great will some be that you will begin to wonder if I have thrown you as

lambs to the lions.

127 In those times, remember the essence of your calling. Do not put more upon yourself than needs be.

128 All that is asked of you, concerning the lives of men and women of the world, can be said by this: help them to remember who they are and help them understand how to live in harmony with the Celestine Light of Elohim that they might inherit the fullness of their birthright from their Father and Mother in Heaven and a joy inside that surpasses all the world has to offer.

129 Remember that every person ever born upon the earth was born in innocence. They came from the Celestine Light, and at the moment of their birth, all are pure Children of Light.

130 But as they gain years, they are molded by the light or darkness that surrounds them. Most that are surrounded by good parents, friends, and teachers who walk in the light become as the light that surrounds them.

131 But those that have darkness around them most often become as the darkness. They are molded by the wicked examples they see and hear as they grow into men and women.

132 The Celestine Light they had at birth grows dim, sometimes until it can no longer be perceived.

133 But know this: the Celestine Light of Elohim still remains at the core of all but the most wicked. They are not unredeemable, merely lost. To show them by precept and example the way back to the light is a stewardship I have given unto you.

134 Even when the Celestine Light is but a faint

glimmer within them, it still calls them to be greater than they are; to do good and live with virtue and honor, even when their life may be just the opposite of that ideal.

135 And always will they know in their heart that they are fighting against themselves when they do evil.

136 It is unto the lost souls that I send you as a sacred stewardship that they may be lost no more.

137 Show them by the example of your life how to live in the Celestine Light and the benefits of health, happiness, and love that abide with you every day because of the light that you embrace.

138 Let them know that the joy of the light is not just for you, but that they too were born Children of Light and can find again that happiness that was lost.

139 Teach them with your words that they can know the paths they must walk to find the Celestine Light again in their lives.

140 When they are ready to be born again, to cast off their old dry skin and take upon them the beauty of the light, then let them repent and be baptized and show their commitment to living the Celestine Light they love.

141 Unto the baptized Children of Light, you are charged to teach the mysteries and the secrets of power I have given to you, as they are prepared and capable of holding them and fulfilling them in stewardship.

142 This then is the essence of your stewardship among the children of men in this life and the next, and all other things that I have asked you to do are a part of this."

143 Many more things Yeshua spoke to them on that day, but these are things that cannot be written but only spoken among the Children of Light.

Light and Darkness

144 On another day, Yeshua elaborated upon good and evil and the light and the darkness that he often referred to, saying, "Because the Children of Light within the communities live in the fullness of the Celestine Light, they will make enemies of both those that live in darkness and even among many of those who live in a part of the light.

145 Those that live in the darkness will hate you because you oppose them.

146 Those that live in a partial light will resent you and despise you because you remind them that they are slaves to their weaknesses, instead of masters over them.

147 Though you will live apart from them, you will still encounter them, and in their own guilt, they will desire to control you and dictate the things in your private and community lives that you can and cannot do.

148 They shall try to force you by law or violence to be like them or be no more, that none would remain whose lives would remind them of the error of their own.

149 They will desire to absorb you into a community of common darkness, where all walk the same wrong path, that they may no longer remember or consider that there was any other choice.

150 With no other choice, they can justify themselves as being just like everyone else. And if that is how everyone is, how could it be wrong?

151 Take heed that you are not caught unaware. At times, the attacks upon your way of life may be strong and blatant.

152 But at other times, they will be subtle and insidious, so slowly eating away at your light that you do not even realize it is diminishing, until you find yourself in a place of great darkness without understanding how you arrived there.

153 But light has nothing to fear from darkness. It is only darkness that needs fear the light.

154 In a battle of good and evil, light will win simply by increasing the light.

155 Darkness is nothing of itself. It has no power; it has no form or substance. Darkness is merely the dimness of light or the void left when light is no longer present.

156 You can bring a light into a dark room, but you can only make a room dark by taking away the light.

157 Darkness can only exist in the absence of light. It can only increase if light diminishes; it can only spread forth across the land if the light capitulates and only win if the light abdicates.

158 But light increases with faith and desire, holding fast to that which you know to be true, and magnifies when it abides in Communities of Light.

159 No darkness, no matter how gloomy or pervasive, can withstand the Celestine Light intent upon overcoming it.

160 Therefore, remember these things and never fear the darkness or the evil intentions of men upon you, for you are the light, and the Celestine Light shall always

have the power to overcome the darkness."

PATHWAY TO EXALTATION

Excerpted from the Oracles of Celestine Light: Vivus: Chapter 99

And it came to pass that Yeshua, Miriam, Salome, and the Apostles returned to the house of the family of Lazarus in Bethany through the same portal they had traveled through to the world of Ferrtho in the Fourth Kingdom.

2 As had happened previously, it seemed to the other family members in Bethany that only mere hours had passed, while to those returning it seemed certain they had been gone many days.

3 Everyone returning from the Fifth Kingdom rested for a day and a night, and the following day Yeshua made an important announcement to his Apostles, saying, "I desire to speak one more time to the Children of Light to help them on their journeys of discovery and personal growth before I leave this world to not return again, save by the spirit within, for their spirits call out to me, and I must give them one more solace."

4 Yeshua sensed that many of his Apostles were saddened contemplating his departure, and he told them, "Do not be sorrowful that the time has come for me to leave this physical world that we have shared. Know that as I leave, you will be propelled into the fullness of your callings, into the majesty of your

potential, and I hope that you will take joy in this.

5 Prepare yourselves now for something you have not experienced in such magnitude, which we shall embark upon after the noonday. Children of Light in every land shall hear my voice speaking to them in their minds, such a thing as most have never conceived. And those who are ready to be numbered among you will heed my words and gather unto you."

6 Later that day, after the noonday meal, Yeshua went with his Apostles, wives, children, and the family of Lazarus to a grove of trees on a nearby hill. A crude bench with the sun shining down upon it had been made out of a long, flat stone set upon two squat stones on either end, and upon this Yeshua sat while everyone else gathered around him, some sitting on the ground and others with their backs against trees.

7 Yeshua closed his eyes, and tilting his head up toward the sun, he held his lower arms up and level, with palms open and facing up. After but a few seconds, his resonant voice came into the minds of all of those sitting near him, even members of the family of Lazarus and many of the children who had never before heard the voice of someone speaking in their mind.

8 And not just those present heard his voice, but every Child of Light in the communities upon Lake Gennesaret also heard his voice at the same instant speaking to them in their minds regardless of what they were doing.

9 And more than this as well, for every Child of Light upon the earth heard the voice of Yeshua speaking to them in their minds at that very moment, causing great

consternation among many. For in far-off lands, many people, though Children of Light in the actions of their lives, had never heard of Yeshua, nor ever imagined a sane man could hear voices in their minds.

10 Yeshua spoke to them all in one voice saying, "Fear not, my brothers and sisters of light. I am Yeshua, your elder brother who has come to earth to illuminate the path of eternity for you.

11 Many of you have never seen my face or heard my voice or even my name spoken upon the lips of men, but you know me in your heart, for we were together before this world was.

12 And I know you, for you are a Child of Light, my brothers and sisters of spirit. It matters not the color of your skin, whether you are male or female, young or old, rich or poor, or the religion you profess. By the good actions of your life, you have been numbered among the Children of Light, and I now call you to come and embrace your true family and the path of greater glory and fulfillment.

13 You live in a world of challenge and much darkness, but that does not mean your life must be an endless challenge or continually dimmed by the darkness of the people and places that surround you.

14 Even if you are a slave, chained to a dais, you can change your thoughts and take yourself in your heart and mind to a place within your essence where resides the spirit of Elohim, and there you will find peace and an abundance of Celestine Light that cannot be taken or dimmed by the world.

15 For those who have their freedom, your thoughts

may be just the beginning of the light you can bathe yourselves in, for your feet can walk and carry you elsewhere to a place where the Celestine Light that comes from God never dims, even to the Communities of Light where you can bask each day in the uplifting spirits, words, and actions of your brothers and sisters of light.

16 This is my call now to every Child of Light upon the earth, wherever you may be: come to the Communities of Light upon Lake Gennesaret in the land of Palestine.

17 Come to the place where your brothers and sisters dwell.

18 Come to the place where the Celestine Light of divinity glows on every face and the darkness of the world can find no place to cast its shadow.

19 Come to the place where harmony reins, where your belly will be full and your life will be fuller.

20 Come to the place of Celestine Light where you will become more than you are and more than you imagined you could be.

21 Where the divine fills your heart and mind, guiding the lives of everyone to greater happiness, health, knowledge, longevity, and spiritual fulfillment.

22 Come to the place where you will be given secret knowledge and the mysteries of all things shall be revealed; that with this knowledge you may go forth in the world but not of it; in it but no longer fearful of it; in it but greater than it.

23 Come to the place of Celestine Light where you will learn the secrets of longevity, where the life of a Child of Light may exceed those of the children of the

world tenfold, as does the knowledge in their minds and the empathy and love in their hearts.

24 I would speak to you now more about longevity, for this is a desirable pursuit, for with greater years you can do greater good.

25 People of the world pursue longevity too, but it is something they will never hold, for they seek only to extend the life of the physical body and longevity can only be obtained by also nourishing the soul.

26 How then is the soul nourished, my brothers and sisters, you who are the Children of Light?

27 It begins with community. Not a community of neighbors and even friends, but a Community of Celestine Light, where all are family, and the love and concern for your neighbor is as great as for your own children.

28 Community then is the foundation of longevity, not the individual or the individual's actions or choices, no matter how good they may be.

29 Good actions of health and diet may add some years to the life of man, but they will not double or triple his lifespan, save he does them nourished in the bosom of the Family of Light.

30 Therefore, I say unto you: put your affairs in order and come now to live among your brothers and sisters in the Communities of Celestine Light upon Lake Gennesaret in the land called Palestine. Though you may not know them, they wait for you, to welcome you home.

31 Fear not the cost, nor the Romans, nor the Greeks or the Persians or the Egyptians or any other people

upon the earth, for the hand of God shall be upon all who make the journey and none shall forbid your passage or slow your way, and whatever money you have shall be sufficient.

32 When you have arrived, you will begin to change. The darkness of the world will fall away, and health and knowledge and joy shall begin to come unto you in abundance.

33 And to all who live in the Communities of Light, both those already there and those still to come, I say unto you: live long, be one, seek out the Celestine Light in all things.

34 There is so much for you to learn and experience that you could never do it in the one short lifetime of the people of the world. Nor would it benefit you to come back in another lifetime, having forgotten everything you learned in the previous and needing to start all over again from the beginning.

35 It is only by living a life two or three or four or even ten times longer than the people of the world, that you can learn all that you need to learn and experience all that you need to experience, to become all that you have the potential to become and do all the good in the world you are capable of doing.

36 Upon the foundation of life within the Community of Light, you can now add the other ingredients of the master recipe of longevity.

37 Consider not just the physical body when you think of longevity, for those who do are doomed to die before they ever taste of the longevity they seek.

38 Your body is the vessel for your eternal soul, your

eternal spirit that cannot be neglected. It is only when these two are nourished equally, within the Community of Celestine Light, that the fullness of longevity can be manifested.

Six-pointed Star of Longevity

39 "The six-pointed star of longevity is this: life in a Community of Celestine Light, physical vibrancy, continual mental expansion, service and empathy to others, spiritual nourishment, and discovering and using the powers of your Xe.

40 There is more to fulfilling each of these than you might imagine. For with each, you must look to perfecting yourselves, to becoming more like the Elohim, to consider how it is you can fulfill the highest potential of the energy, not wallow in the lowest.

Point One: Community of Light

41 "The simplest would seem to be to live in the Community of Celestine Light; but living there is not the same as being alive there, and being alive is what you must be: alive in the fullness of the teachings of Elohim, lived faithfully in your life; alive by being a very active and contributing member of the community, not a hermit in your house; alive by relishing and loving the Family of Light to which you are a part.

Point Two: Physical Vibrancy

42 "So physical vibrancy would seem to be straightforward, for the teachings of diet and healthy lifestyle have been given to you in detail. But physical vibrancy is more than diet and exercise. It is so much a fulfillment of the word vibrant.

43 Are you sweet of disposition? Do you judge none,

including yourself? Do you speak ill words of none and gossip not at all about others? When you speak to friends and family, is it only in praise and never with an uninvited or subtle criticism? Do you laugh easily and smile often? Do you whistle and sing happy tunes, even while you work? Do you make your home a piece of Heaven by the ambience you create and the example you set by the things you say and do?

44 And the physical aspect of longevity is still much more than this. Your Vm plays a vital role in the physical aspect of your longevity. It should be activated daily throughout your life, even when you are alone, but not in the crude and debasing ways of the world, nor is a culmination necessary or even any connection to things sexual, for there is much more to the energy of the Vm than that. And with this, you learn one of the secrets within the secrets of longevity.

45 The essence of your Vm is a very sacred power, even the power to create life, but includes other wonderful creations as well. It is castrated when it is used in worldly ways only for physical pleasure or sullied by debasing language or illicit thoughts.

46 Nevertheless, within the sanctity of your marriage, you have great latitude with respect to how you give and receive pleasure through your Vms. All is well if what you do strengthens your bonds together. But be certain that it does. And understand clearly that physically pleasuring your Vms in the debased ways of the world will not add to the length of your days, but doing so with love within your marriage will.

47 To achieve physical vibrancy and longevity when

physically stimulating your Vms, you must do so within the realm of sacredness and only within the bonds of marriage publicly proclaimed. Seek to become blissfully lost in the wonder of Celestine Love, without crude words or disrespectful actions, but focusing only on one another and pleasure mutually given and received.

48 It matters not the composition of your marriage to other Children of Light, be it one man and one woman or two women or two men or a mixture of a man and women, or a woman and men. What is important is the depth of your love evidenced by the steadfastness of your commitment and the exclusivity and sacredness of your unions.

49 But let none among you be fornicators or adulterers, for this is the spirit of darkness and the world.

50 And may all among you be open and accepting of the vows of fidelity and commitment given in marriage by any of your brothers and sisters of the Celestine Light, in whatever arrangement of love among one another that they choose.

51 Beyond that, remember the secret within the secret.

Point Three: Expansion of the Mind

52 "What then of the aspect of the mind? Is it just ever pursuing greater knowledge? A worthy endeavor to be sure, one that all Children of Light should seek every year of their life. But there is much more to this aspect.

53 What is it you are learning? Is it about the latest fashions in the cities or learning how to create the

clothes? Is it watching the street dancers or learning the dance? Is it marveling at great art or practicing to become a great artist? You can do the former as long as you also choose to do some of the latter that expands your creativity. But the former without the latter contributes naught to your longevity.

54 Nor is learning only concerned with matters in the Ka. For the Ka and the Ja are intimately connected. What affects one profoundly affects the other.

55 Therefore take heed about what your eyes see and what your ears hear.

56 Seek things that uplift and inspire rather than belittle and disparage.

57 Seek things that warm your heart and calm your mind, not things that cause fear or anxiety.

58 Seek association with situations, places, and people that make you want to become more than you are, not encourage you to be less.

59 Seek out that which is light and calls you to your greatness. And turn away from everyone and everything that does not.

Point Four: Service to Others

60 "And what does it mean to serve others? It is not just giving alms for the poor or to support the community or worthy institutions.

61 Money is but a token that is both helpful and appreciated, but true service requires your participation.

62 So true this is—that you can consider the wages from a day's work donated to a worthy cause of less value than one hour of your time given in sweetness to the same cause.

63 True service is when one who is stronger, be it physically, mentally, financially, emotionally, or spiritually, comes to one who is weaker, in humility, and serves them to their happiness with respect and kindness.

64 This is the service a man gives to his wife, when he seeks her joy before his and does as she asks in giving intimate pleasures.

65 This is the service a mother gives to her children when she counsels and cajoles rather than commands and does not force her will upon them.

66 This is the service those of greater means give to those of lesser when they rise with the first sun to work side by side and help them build a house, rather than donate alms in a minute and have the matter forgotten.

67 This is the service of the ruler who listens to the will of the people rather than imposing his own will upon them, even when he disagrees with that which the people call to be done.

68 These are the services and others like unto them that build Communities of Celestine Light, instead of just communities of friends, acquaintances, and coworkers.

Point Five: Spiritual Nourishment

69 "In the world, among the Ganish of all persuasions, it is thought that to be nourished spiritually is to learn more of their faith and to live it more faithfully. Alone, this is just partial nourishment, like unto the mother who feeds her children in the morning but not in the afternoon or evening.

70 Like service to others, spiritual nourishment in

fullness is more than you.

71 To be filled, you must commune with others of your faith. You must share your experiences and knowledge with those who have less experience and knowledge and avidly seek out and learn from those who have more.

72 Therefore, know with certainty that spiritual nourishment is much more than what you learn that is written on a scroll, even much more than my words set down by a scribe.

73 Spiritual nourishment is an unquenchable thirst and curiosity about what you do not know, fulfilled as much by what you learn from others and what you teach to others as by what you learn from reading the words written on a scroll.

74 Remember, all points of the six-sided star, concerning seeking the higher path when a choice is before you, not the lower.

Point Six: Discovering the Powers of Your Xe

75 "Your time upon this earth is very finite. You know not when the last day shall be. Perhaps even now you will breathe your last breath in the physical life. Therefore, do not squander time, which is a commodity more precious than gold or jewels.

76 More than this, live your life to increase its length, rather than abuse your life, shortening its days.

77 Many religions teach that your days are numbered before you ever are born. But I say unto you: this is not true.

78 Based upon how you live, the Elohim know the exact day you shall leave the physical life. But you are

the master of you, and that day is not written in stone.

79 If you choose to live differently, to live better, healthier, smarter, more in balance with the aeon of life, more in harmony with the Celestine spirit of the Elohim, then you lengthen your days upon the earth.

80 Elohim still knows the very day that shall be your last in the physical life, but your actions have moved the day and it is not the same day that it was. And you can continue to move it, adding more and more years to do good, even until you have lived for one thousand years upon the earth.

81 But remember, remember, that even as good actions move the day further away in time, so do bad actions bring it closer.

82 All the things I have spoken about contribute to the lengthening of your days. But there is one more thing, often forgotten or unknown by many, that has as vital a role as any other, and that is discovering and using the powers of your Xe.

83 The physical men and women that you see all around you, probably even in yourself or your beloved, are not the men and women that can be.

84 You were endowed with gifts of Celestine Light before you were born into this life: the power to hear when others have not spoken, the power to travel from one place to another without traveling, the power to levitate objects and yourself, the power to make fire by calling the aeon and focusing it in your hands, and many, many other powers of Celestine Light have you been gifted with.

85 Until you discover these gifts and can use them,

you are but a cripple. Until you can discover these gifts and use them, your life will come and go just like any other person upon this world, for until you discover and use these gifts, you are still like the people of this world and are bound by their beliefs of mortality.

86 But to discover the secrets of these gifts is not something that can be done in solitude. Nor for many can it be done in days or months or years.

87 Knowing the secrets of your Xe and how to use them releases the aeons of Celestine Light upon you, and this shall add as many days to your physical life as all the other things you can do.

88 Each day, there are hours to sleep and eat and work and a precious few remaining for you to choose to do with them as you wish.

89 If you choose to spend them rather than invest them, to squander them on mindless entertainment or time lost doing nothing, then nothing is what you shall inherit, both in this life and the life to come.

90 Your time is precious, more than gold or jewels. Invest it in becoming more than you are in every way and your investment shall reward you in every way as your years upon the earth lengthen.

91 While king after king after king passes away and their Kingdoms too, you shall remain. And more good shall be done upon the earth than if you had returned for one hundred lifetimes.

Mind the Bridge upon Which You Stand

92 "Please consider that each of you stand on a bridge that leads to other Children of Light.

93 On one side of the bridge are the Children of

Light who have more knowledge and experience than you. These are your mentors and teachers to help you grow and expand in the Celestine Light of the Elohim.

94 Look to them often that you may gain a greater understanding of all things. Observe what they do and how they do it, how they pray, how they work, how they call and use their Celestine gifts of power, and how they speak and treat others, both Children of Light and the Ganish.

95 Do not hesitate to inquire of them when you seek an understanding of all things Celestine. Of course, they will help you, for you are all here to serve one another with love.

96 On the other side of the bridge are the Children of Light who have less knowledge and experience than you. You are the one who stands at the other end of their bridge as their mentor and teacher.

97 Even as you look to those with greater knowledge and experience, so those at the other end of your bridge look to you to help them gain a greater understanding of the Celestine Light.

98 Know that this is a sacred duty to which you are called all of your life: to faithfully be an example of the Celestine Light to all those who see your life and to share your knowledge and experiences with all Children of Light who ask of you or to whom you are called to teach.

99 Therefore, always remember that you are on a bridge crossing the great chasm of the world. To the right, anchoring that side, are those that teach you by precept and example. To the left, anchoring that side, are those that you teach by precept and example.

100 Both sides are needed to safely anchor the bridge to insure it does not give way and fall into the chasm of the world. Therefore, gratefully seek out your mentors and teachers and, with humility, be willing to be a mentor and teacher to those who look to you for greater understanding and knowledge.

The Foundations of the Community of Light

101 "How are the communities of Celestine Light different than any other community upon the earth?

102 They are different because they are not just a grouping of like-minded people, but the unity of a Family of Light, where the love for everyone is as family, not just friends.

103 They are different because they are in the world, but not of it, and in their cloistered locations, not even in it very much.

104 They are different because the members live according to the health and diet teachings of Celestine Light, resulting in fulfilling lives of joy and happiness, with little sickness or disease and with years upon the earth far in excess of the people of the world.

105 They are different because everyone is a servant to all others, and none is a master to any.

106 They are different because they are neither patriarchal in nature, nor matriarchal, but are led in the temporal by the elders, both men and women, with the most knowledge, experience, and abilities of all things temporal and in the spiritual by the Apostles, both men and women, called because of their knowledge, experience, and abilities in the gifts, powers, and responsibilities of the Celestine Light.

107 They are different because that which is considered magic, fantasy, and impossible among the people of the world is normal and common among the Children of Light.

108 They are different because in a world where most people live in poverty, the Children of Light create self-sufficient abundance.

109 They are different because they are filled with hope not despair, with faith not doubt, with love not hate, with smiles not frowns, with easy forgiveness not quick judgment, with working together not at odds, with self-confidence not self-pity, with unity not divisiveness, with acceptance of differences not prejudice, with words of praise not criticisms, with purpose not aimlessness.

Prophecy of the Days to Come

110 "Now I would give you some last words, my brothers and sisters of this generation. I have spoken many things to the Children of Light over the years I have walked in the flesh upon this earth. Some of you have been with me for many of those years, while others are hearing my voice now for the very first time.

111 My words have been written for the Children of Light. They are for you who hear my voice as I speak to you now.

112 I will give no more new to you, for all you need to gain exaltation and eternal life I have already spoken. Now it is you who must take it upon yourselves to know and live that which I have spoken.

113 And those that know and live my words shall be no more of this earth, even though their feet may still tread upon it. For those who know and live my words

shall be more than men and more than women. They shall be Celestines, who, staying steadfast in the light, shall someday become Adepts against whom the fiery darts of the adversary within have no persuasion, the forces of the world be they army or king, have no power, and to whom the body is the servant not the master.

114 But your time on the earth is short. You are few, and the Ganish are many. Gather now to one another at Lake Gennesaret and live together and prosper as long as the world will let you.

115 Grow and expand yourself in the ways of the Celestine Light of Elohim. Learn the secrets I have given unto my Apostles to teach unto you. Become Adepts of the Celestine Light, each and every one of you, that the people of the world may have no power over you, for you will be one with the Celestine Light and the Celestine Light shall be one with you.

116 When the world hates you, and they shall, when they seek to destroy you, and they shall, defend yourselves and your families when you must by whatever means you have, but seek not confrontation.

117 Be willing to burn your homes and farms and boats and depart from the land, if it will save the spilling of blood, either yours or the Ganish's who persecute you.

118 But do not surrender to them or put yourselves willingly into their hands, save you are an Adept over which they can have no real power, only imagined. And great shall be their surprise when that misconception is revealed.

119 Those of you who are just beginning to walk

the path of Celestine Light seek the protection of the Adepts. When the peace and bliss of your communities is broken by the jealous people of the world who think to take that which they have not earned, leave them stubble and ash and withdraw from the land to the sanctuary that shall be revealed by the Elohim to my Apostles.

120 And it shall be that you shall continue to grow in the Celestine Light. Under the trials and tribulations, you shall become more than you were until the earth can no longer hold you in its thickness, for you will be of the light.

121 On that day, this generation shall rise up without tasting death, even as the people of Enoch, and I shall meet you in the sky and show you the way to the heavenly glory that awaits the faithful Children of Light, even you, my dear brothers and sisters.

122 When you are no more upon the earth, the fullness of Celestine Light shall be taken from it for two thousand years, save from those who remain as earth Stewards, and the Ganish shall wander in the darkness they created.

123 But each new generation born upon the earth shall have more souls who humbly and sincerely seek the light that is not there in the world, but flourishes in their hearts and manifests in their lives.

The Generation of Promise

124 "Therefore, the Celestine Light shall grow again upon the earth, generation upon generation, until two thousand years have passed. Then there shall be sufficient light upon the earth that once again the Celestine Light

shall be reborn, and upon this day begins a new era as the Generation of Promise is also born.

125 Unto the Generation of Promise will be given all that has been given to you, for on that day, there will be more Children of Light upon the earth than there are people in all the world today.

126 They shall hunger for the light, and it shall be given to them in fullness, and Adepts of knowledge and power shall walk the world once more to protect it from those that still remain in darkness.

127 Were the Adepts not to come, it would be the end of the world, for the leaders of great countries and those not so great will have the power to destroy all life, and this they will do, save the Adepts of Celestine Light join as one with the other Children of Light to stop the travesty.

128 For when the power of the light unites as one, the darkness has no place to be. Darkness of itself is nothing, but the absence of the light. When the light asserts its place in brilliance, the darkness is no more.

Final Words

129 "And of all the words I have said to you, my brothers and sisters, these I say to you last: Love one another, even as I have loved you. In this is all the power of creation, all the power of the Elohim, and all the potential of the Celestine Light that is within you, waiting to shine unto the world."

INDEX

B

E

I

K

L

M

Milton Keynes UK
Ingram Content Group UK Ltd.
UKHW040126091223
433996UK00001BA/10

9 780938 001201